Brave Awareness

Brave Awareness:

The Practice of Being Okay Even When Life Isn't

by Ronn Pawo McLane

Brave Awareness: The Practice of Being Okay Even When Life Isn't

First Edition, 2026

ISBN: 979-8-9949366-0-3

Printed in the United States of America

Dedication:

To the one who stayed when it was hard to stay.

Who listened inward when no one else could hear.

Who whispered, "Keep going", even when the world offered silence.

This is for me.

And it is for you, too, if you have ever been the only one cheering

yourself on.

May these words feel like a hand on your back, saying:

You are not alone. You are not wrong. You are not broken.

Author's Note: A Letter to Those Who Know Me

If you find yourself on these pages, by name or by story, I want you to know this:

I did not author this book to accuse, blame, or shame anyone. I wrote it to tell the truth of my experience to reclaim it, reflect on it, and allow it to be seen without needing it to be validated by others.

This book is not the whole truth. It is my truth shaped by memory, emotion, and the process of healing. It is one thread of many, pulled through the years with care, grief, growth, and love.

Some of what I share may feel uncomfortable, especially for those who lived through parts of it with me. That discomfort is not a formal accusation. It is an invitation to witness how our lives intertwined, how wounds were formed, and how wholeness began.

Please know I have carried these stories silently for a long time. Writing them was an act of integration, not retaliation.

We do not all have to remember things the same way. But I believe there is power and peace in telling the truth as we experienced it.

With compassion and clarity,

Ronn

Table of Contents

A Note to the Reader on Practice and Safety

The practices and insights in this book are based on my personal experience, my training as a meditation teacher, and my deep belief in the power of awareness to transform our lives. This book is intended as an educational and inspirational resource to support your journey of self-discovery.

It is not, however, a substitute for professional medical or psychological treatment. The path of looking inward can be challenging, and for individuals with a history of severe mental health conditions, including but not limited to psychosis, schizophrenia, or severe trauma, some mindfulness and meditation practices may be contraindicated without the guidance of a qualified healthcare professional.

If you have a serious mental health condition or are in crisis, please consult with your doctor or a licensed therapist to determine if the practices in this book are appropriate for you at this time. Your safety and well-being are paramount. This journey is about befriending yourself, and the wisest first step is always to ensure you have the right support system in place.

Preface

The Year Everything Stopped Making Sense

I remember a year, not so long ago, that started with a feeling of absolute triumph. I was riding high, convinced I had finally wrestled the tiger by the tail. It felt cosmic, almost destined, that this was *my* year. I even marked it permanently, by getting a tattoo of my lucky number nine, the Roman numeral IX, placed on my left shoulder on the ninth day of the ninth month in a year ending with nine. I felt so in control. I had extricated myself from what felt like a terribly toxic relationship and was set up for my continued career success. I was rocking and rolling.

Then, the first crack appeared. It was not a slow erosion; it was a sudden, shocking blow: I got fired from my dream job. The company, the people I worked with were like family. For years, I had been their *"Ronn-inator"*, single-handedly shaping their marketing and group sales, even teaching data analysis to corporate finance teams and advertising agencies. I was praised, rewarded, and presented as a model of achievement. And then, in an instant, I was cast out like garbage. The people I thought were my closest colleagues and friends, every single one of them fled. They distanced themselves from me as if I were a pariah. The hurt of that betrayal, the shock, the disbelief, the total confusion, and the anger, I can still feel it.

My long-term relationship, a decade-long connection where we had been each other's champions and fostered mutual career growth, was also unraveling. Though we had broken up several weeks before my being fired, he was still in my orbit, still offering supportive words, determined that I would bounce back quickly. But even as I pushed forward, the world continued to tilt. I tried to pivot, hanging out my shingle as a consultant, convinced my unique expertise would immediately land clients. I even hired a former colleague. But no clients ever materialized. The financial drain began slowly at first, then sped up. My savings dwindled. The lawyer secured a small settlement in compensation, providing a temporary reprieve, but the pressure mounted.

Then came the housing crisis. Our mortgage with Bank of America doubled, and we were locked in a bitter battle over the ownership of the home that I had meticulously remodeled and loved. Someone advised me to withhold payments to force renegotiation, but with no income, I could not refinance in my name. The bank moved to foreclose. I discovered a loophole, albeit a costly one, that enabled me to sell the house within 90 days and keep some profit, but it was a desperate act, and at closing, my ex demanded half of the proceeds, or he would not sign.

I had never felt so utterly beaten. My money was gone, my relationship failed, and my career was nonexistent. My identity, everything I thought I was, was crumbling away. I had been relying heavily on my sister and mother for emotional support, but even their patience was wearing thin. My sister would not pick up my calls, and my mother, a covert narcissist, offered little solace. I felt completely trapped, broken, and defeated.

A plan formed itself in that abyss. I did not want a gruesome death. I just could not see how I was ever going to support myself, how I was going to survive. So, I planned to use the very last of my dwindling funds to go to a Party City, intending to buy a small canister of helium to suffocate myself quickly. I had just enough money. As a last desperate effort, I called a suicide prevention line. The response was a gross disappointment; someone briefly listened and then vaguely told me it would get better and to hang in there. It offered no comfort, no anchor.

On the morning that I was going to get the helium, my friend Brent from the Buddhist temple called. "Hey," he said, "I have been worried about you. Can I take you to lunch today and talk?" Despite having no appetite, I really liked Brent, and I agreed. He arrived quickly, just as I was getting out of the shower. I dressed, and he drove me to a nearby Panera Bread, a place where I had spent countless hours. In line, Brent stepped up, placed his order, swiped his card, and walked away to the drink station. He absentmindedly left me to order without paying for my lunch. The rest of that lunch was a blur. My mind screamed at me, trapped in a loop: I had just spent a chunk of the money I needed for the helium on lunch I did not have the stomach to eat. My plan was sunk. I could not even do *that* right. After that, I went home and collapsed, sleeping on and off for days. I do not remember eating or drinking, but my best friend, Nikia, my all-white, blue-eyed Siberian husky, remained near me, letting me know when she needed to go out. She always had food and water, but I had collapsed mentally and physically. I truly felt I had failed at everything, even in the simple act of ending my suffering.

But at that absolute lowest point, something shifted. It felt like the death of a lot of things for me, and when I woke up days later, I had a different outlook. I had lost everything that I had worked so hard for, and I was still alive. I leaned heavily into my meditation practice and frequently visited the Buddhist temple, where an amazing community quickly embraced me and soon made me a leader. During that time, I met Lama Surya Das and began working with him. Things were definitely starting to make a turn. I was supporting myself financially again, had filed for bankruptcy, sold the house, and moved into an apartment, living a calmer, more peaceful existence. I felt lighter and calmer than I had felt in years. I was not sweating the small stuff, and in fact, I was finding joy in the little things. I remember starting a gratitude journal, and all I could put on that first page was peanut butter and jelly and my dog Nikia. But slowly, I was finding joy and appreciation in my cup of tea, the taste of cheese, and a sunset. I was sleeping comfortably and opening up spiritually. It was during this time that I was also being introduced to the teachings of Dzogchen and Mahamudra. I had been stripped bare and then was filled back up with this profound understanding.

This was the turning point that led to now. It was the basis for the changes toward a mindful, aware life. A shift guided by a core teaching from a text written by Lama Surya Das: *"In the ultimate sense, nothing matters, and in the relative sense, where we live, everything matters."* This became the key to understanding that these two truths exist simultaneously as a whole. I am not separate, even when I feel like I am. There is another teaching: *"Do not be like a dog chasing after every thrown stick or bone. Instead, be like a lion and jump directly onto the thrower."* This taught me not to be distracted by the small stuff, but to look directly into what matters and focus my awareness. Stripping my experiences of the illusion of their material and relational attachments showed me I was not separate; I could not possibly be separate. This profound period of unraveling and rebuilding, following my decades of meditation practice, eventually led me to a six-part journey of ketamine-assisted therapy, where the insights and teachings I had absorbed were reorganized in my brain differently. It was there that I could truly see what was going on and contributing to my constant waves of suffering.

Introduction: The Fear We Cannot Name

Suffering is not just pain. It is not just sadness, grief, or loss. At its core, suffering is fear. Not the obvious kind, the fear of heights, the fear of public speaking, or the fear of spiders. No, this fear is deeper, more insidious. It is the fear that we are not enough. The fear of never achieving our true desires. The fear that we will lose what we love. Ultimately, the fear is that none of this will matter.

Most of us do not recognize this fear because it does not always show up as panic or terror. It wears different masks. Sometimes it looks like ambition, the endless chase to achieve more, to prove our worth, to finally be enough. Sometimes it looks like overthinking, replaying conversations in our heads, scanning for mistakes, and making sure we did not say the wrong thing. Sometimes it looks like anger, because if we are in control, if we are right, if we are strong, then maybe we will not feel small, lost, or vulnerable. And sometimes, this fear shows up as doubt.

Doubt that this path, this practice, or this book will work. Doubt that peace is possible for someone like me. Doubt that awareness will make a difference.

I have lived inside this fear for most of my life. It has followed me like a shadow, whispering that no matter what I do, I will never fully get it right. That happiness is something I must chase. That peace is something fragile, easily lost. And so, for years, I did what everyone does: I tried to outrun the fear. I worked harder, achieved more, controlled what I could, and numbed what I could not. But no matter how much I accomplished, how many good things happened, the fear was still there, waiting. And it was exhausting.

The truth is, we are wired for fear. Our ancestors had to be. The humans who stayed hyper-aware of threats, of wild animals, of rival tribes, of starvation, were the ones who survived. Their nervous systems stayed on high alert, their minds constantly scanning for danger. And now, thousands of years later, that same survival system still runs in us.

Only now, the danger is not a predator in the bushes. It is a missed email. A financial setback. A conversation gone wrong. It is feeling unseen, feeling unloved, feeling like we do not belong.

We do not recognize this fear for what it is because it is so embedded in the fabric of our lives. It feels normal. Expected. Unavoidable. But if we look closely, we begin to see something profound. Everything we suffer over is something we are afraid of losing. We love someone. We are afraid of their absence. We succeed. We fear that failure is looming. We feel happy. We fear that moment will pass, and sadness will come.

We are trapped in this cycle: attachment, loss, craving, resistance. A constant, unconscious fight to hold onto what feels good and push away what feels bad. A fight we will never, ever win. Because nothing, not one single thing, is permanent.

The Trap of Wanting and Clinging

It is not just fear of losing what we have. It is the desperate, aching hunger for what we think we need to be happy. We are taught to believe that peace, fulfillment, and worthiness are things we must earn. That they come from the outside. That we need to get more, more love, more money, more success, more validation. But the second we get the thing we wanted, something else takes its place. Desire never ends.

If you have ever tried to "manifest" your way into happiness, you know this to be true. We are told that if we think positively, if we visualize hard enough, if we align with the universe, we will get what we want. And maybe, for a while, we do. Maybe we will land the job, attract the partner, and hit the goal.

But it does not end the suffering. Because the suffering was never about the thing. It was about our belief that we needed everything to be okay. This is why so many people, people who "have it all", are still miserable. Wealthy people still feel insecure. Famous people still feel unworthy. People in relationships still feel lonely. The problem was never about getting what we wanted. The problem was believing that we were incomplete without it.

And so, we keep chasing. We keep grasping. We continue to live with an unshakable feeling that something is missing, never realizing that the "missing" feeling is actually manufactured by the mind itself.

Seeing Through the Illusion: Why Nothing Is Real

What if I told you that none of this is real? Not in the way you think it is.

Think about money. Money is a powerful force in our lives. It dictates where we live, what we eat, and how much freedom we feel we have. It has caused wars. It has destroyed relationships. It is the reason people wake up in the morning and the reason they lose sleep at night. And yet, money is a concept, an agreed-upon system. The bills in your wallet are just printed paper. The numbers in your bank account are a digital code. Their value exists only because we collectively believe that it does. The moment that belief shifts, the entire system crumbles. But we do not question it. We function as if it is real, as if it means something inherent, as if it is an external truth rather than an internal agreement.

Now, extend that to success. What is success? Is it a certain salary? A title? A level of recognition? Who decides? Where is the finish line? If success were real, an absolute truth, then it would be the same for everyone. But it is not. It is a moving target, a shifting goalpost, a definition that changes depending on who you ask, the era in which you live, and the values you hold.

And what about ownership? You own nothing. Not really. The house you call yours. It will belong to someone else one day. The clothes you wear. They will fray, be discarded, and return to the earth. Even your body is borrowed. Cells are aging, skin is changing, and bones are weakening. No matter how much you try to hold onto it, nothing in this world is truly yours.

So, if money is not real, success is not real, and ownership is not absolute, then what exactly are we suffering over? We suffer because we believe these things are real. We treat them as fixed truths rather than shifting illusions. We suffer because we are conditioned to chase things that were never solid to begin with. And the most painful illusion of all? The idea that we can control any of it.

What if the things we suffer over are not actually real? What if they are nothing more than shifting illusions, constructs that dissolve the moment we stop gripping them so tightly? We move through life as if these ideas, money, success, time, and ownership are fixed realities, as if they exist outside of us and dictate the course of our lives. But what if they are just agreements? Stories we have been told and continue to tell ourselves? What if suffering is not caused by the things we lack or the things we lose, but by our refusal to accept their impermanence? Because here is the thing: Nothing is missing. The moment we stop measuring our worth by what we have acquired, the moment we stop believing that happiness lives in the next achievement, the next relationship, the next goal, and we begin to see what has always been true: peace is already here. We have been searching for something that was never lost. But because we were taught to look outside of ourselves, we missed it. We missed the quiet stillness in the spaces between thoughts. We missed the feeling of wholeness that arises in a single, deep breath. We missed the profound relief of simply being, without needing anything to be different. We missed life as it was happening. Because we were too busy chasing a version of life that we thought we needed.

A Note on the Word "Radical"

A quick note on a word I use frequently throughout this book: **radical**. In today's charged climate, this word is often used to mean "extreme" or is associated with a battle. That is not the sense in which it is used here.

I use "radical" in its truest, original sense, from the Latin *radix*, meaning **"root."** A radical change is one that gets to the root of the matter. The practices in this book are radical not because they are aggressive, but because they represent a fundamental departure from the patterned reactivity that governs so much of our suffering. It is a gentle but profound return to the root of our own being.

Radical Neutrality: The Space Between Craving and Aversion

So, what do we do with all of this? If suffering is fueled by craving and fear, then what is the way out?

Most spiritual traditions emphasize the importance of letting go, but people often misunderstand what that entails. Letting go is not about giving up, walking away, or shutting down our emotions. It is not

about pretending we do not care. Letting go is not about detachment;
it is about freedom.

It is about seeing the world as it is: impermanent, interconnected, and
ultimately uncontrollable. It is realizing that happiness is not the goal;
peace is. And peace is not found in grasping, chasing, or controlling. It
is found in accepting things as they are.

This is what I call Radical Neutrality. It is the space between craving
and aversion. The space between clinging and rejection. The place
where suffering ends because we stop resisting reality.

Radical Neutrality is not indifference. It is not passive. It does not
mean withdrawing from life or becoming numb to experiences.
Instead, it is a profound openness to what is, without the compulsion
to change it. It means experiencing both joy and sorrow without
clinging to either. It means walking through the world with awareness,
seeing clearly that all things rise and fall, come and go. This is where
liberation begins, not in controlling life but in releasing the illusion
that we need to.

The Invitation: A New Way of Seeing

This book is not about fixing yourself. You are not broken.

It is not about adding something new to your life. You do not need more.

It is about seeing through the illusion that keeps you suffering. It is about noticing the patterns that control your mind. It is about shifting your perspective so that you can experience life without the weight of constant fear. Because the truth is, you do not need to chase anything. You do not need to change who you are.

You need to wake up to what you already are.

In the chapters ahead, we will explore how to see, understand, and release the conditioned patterns that keep us stuck. We will break down the illusion of suffering and introduce tools for finding deep, lasting peace. Not through blind positivity or spiritual bypassing. Through clarity. Through awareness. Through Radical Neutrality. Are you ready? Then let us begin.

Chapter 1: Seeing the Forest Beyond the Trees

Suffering is a universal experience. It does not matter who you are, where you live, or what you believe; every human life contains some form of discomfort, dissatisfaction, or longing. Sometimes, suffering arrives as an undeniable force: the pain of loss, the weight of grief, or the sting of failure. However, more often, it is subtle, an undercurrent that runs beneath our daily lives. It whispers in the background during moments of waiting, anticipation, or disappointment. It even slips into moments of joy, casting a shadow in the form of worry or attachment. We experience this pull of liking and disliking in nearly every interaction. When we enjoy something, we crave its continuation and fear its loss. When we dislike something, we crave its end and resist its presence. This subtle push and pull may seem harmless, but it shapes how we relate to the present moment, often creating dissatisfaction even in the midst of pleasure.

The Forest of Habitual Patterns

The truth is, we often fail to see how deeply we are entangled in patterns of craving and resistance. Instead of seeing the forest for what it is, a complex ecosystem of our emotions, thoughts, and reactions, we focus on individual trees, mistaking each moment of discomfort or craving as isolated and unrelated. But these small moments add up to a life shaped by resistance to what is and attachment to what we wish would last. We can liken this to walking through a dense forest without a map. Each tree represents a moment of craving or resistance. Instead of observing our surroundings with curiosity and presence, we hyper-focus on one obstacle, one feeling, or one desire at a time. We may spend hours lost in frustration over things that did not go our way or clinging to the fleeting happiness of something we fear will end.

I have seen this confusion firsthand in my role as a Buddhist teacher. One of the teachings that tends to challenge people the most is the idea of suffering. When I would explain that suffering touches every aspect of our lives, students would often push back and insist, "I do not suffer." They associated suffering with dramatic hardship and believed that if they were comfortable and their needs were met, they were free from it. But suffering is not always dramatic; it can be the restless craving for recognition, the discomfort of boredom, or the silent pressure to hold on to a moment of happiness. I remember one student who insisted he was content because his life was simple and predictable. Yet, as we spoke, he confessed that he felt frustrated when even minor disruptions, like traffic or an unexpected request, threw him off balance. That frustration, I explained, was a form of suffering born from resistance to what is. Once he saw it that way, he began to understand that suffering is not about extreme pain; it is about the moments when we resist the reality of life.

Just last week, while having dinner with my husband and some friends, one friend told me they did not really understand meditation. They said they just did not have "that kind of stress" and did not need it. At the same time, I watched them drink their fifth or sixth cocktail of the night. Their comment was a vivid example of how easily we can dismiss our discomfort, even as we are unconsciously seeking ways to manage it.

My Path Through Discomfort: Early Lessons in Awareness

I know this cycle intimately because I have experienced suffering from an early age. When I was 13 years old, I was hospitalized because of severe migraine headaches that I had experienced since the age of two. At that point, the migraines had begun to affect my vision, and I often felt a dizzy, disorienting sensation as though I might pass out. It seemed certain conditions made them worse, particularly heat. I think I spent the first 30 years of my life in a state of being too hot. When I was a kid, we did not have central air conditioning, and my parents would turn off the window units at night. When a headache started, my first instinct was to find a cool place. I would lie on my bunk bed, pointing a small, two-speed white plastic fan towards my face, often with a wet washcloth across my eyes to block light and cool me down. I remember vividly how restless I was, unable to get comfortable or cool down, feeling the headache increase and increase. A migraine for me is akin to the sensation of getting that brain freeze feeling when eating ice cream – a terrible pressure in my head and neck. My eyes ached, and even my teeth hurt, causing a great deal of tension. The experience of finding no comfort, tossing, and turning, trying to find some futile way to relieve the pain, was overwhelming. I just wanted it to end, and it would not. The panic that accompanied the pain often made it worse, a crushing sensation that mirrored the physical ache. During one appointment, I met with a psychiatrist who recorded a cassette tape for me, an early form of what we might now call guided meditation, though it was framed as hypnosis. I was instructed to play this tape in a quiet environment whenever I felt a migraine coming on. When I used the tape, it was something to focus on that distracted me from the pain and discomfort. I still had the little fan and the wet cloth, but I could calm down listening to the Doctor's familiar voice walking me gently through a pattern that I already knew and knew would help ease me. Most of the time, I would relax enough to fall asleep and often wake up a few hours later feeling much better.

The practice did not make the migraines disappear, but something surprising happened: the panic that often accompanied the pain began to ease. Listening to the tape gave me a sense of control, not over the pain itself, but over my response to it. Over time, I learned to separate suffering from pain. The pain was inevitable, but the suffering, the fear, the panic, the stories my mind told, were something I could work with. That experience marked the beginning of my journey into the world of mindfulness and meditation. What struck me most was that practice did not require me to change the external conditions of my life. I was not given a cure for the migraines, but I was given something just as powerful, a way to remain steady in the face of discomfort. This early lesson shaped my understanding of awareness as a tool for acceptance, not control.

The Brave Awareness Solution: Noticing and Radical Neutrality

This journey, often marked by unexpected turns and profound discomfort, consistently brought me back to one fundamental truth: the importance of **awareness**. Awareness begins simply with **noticing**. We are so accustomed to just reacting that we consistently find ourselves at the bottom of a slippery slope before we even realize how we got there. Changing our experience requires us to cultivate the active act of noticing our moods, physical and mental discomforts, as well as joy, pleasure, happiness, and patterned reactivity. Noticing brings us to conscious awareness, where we can actively participate in the experience instead of being dragged around by unconscious, conditioned reactivity.

Discomfort, in all forms, is an inescapable part of life. It arrives as fear, physical heaviness, or emotional agitation. However, through awareness, we learn to observe these experiences without judgment or panic. Awareness creates space. It allows us to witness what arises rather than be overwhelmed by it. Instead of tightening around discomfort or trying to push it away, we can soften and anchor ourselves in the present moment. This perspective offers not only relief from suffering but also a balanced way to experience life as it unfolds.

Awareness is not a shield that blocks discomfort but a lens that clarifies our responses. This clarity fundamentally shifts our relationship with ourselves: we stop having the critical relationship of telling ourselves we aren't enough, or worse, that we are "a work in progress." We stop reaffirming that we are broken, or "sinners," or deficient. Whether during a panic attack or in facing criticism, returning to breath and body provides me with a steady place to stand. This insight showed that I could remain present through waves of fear and heaviness without losing myself. Often, we mistake the presence of discomfort as a sign that something is wrong, that if we feel fear or sadness, we have failed in some way. But discomfort is not a failure; it is a natural part of being human. Awareness helps us shift from reacting to discomfort with resistance to acknowledging it with open compassion.

This understanding of awareness is the bedrock of what I call "Brave Awareness," a path anchored in a five-step model. This foundational

"Awareness" is the very first "A" in the 5A Model. It allows us to begin seeing clearly, and this initial step then opens the door for us to acknowledge what we see, name it, and move toward a compassionate acceptance of our human experience.

Integrating Brave Awareness into My Story: From Experience to Embodiment

For me, integrating Brave Awareness has been a process of consistently "noticing." I am frequently checking in with myself when I feel discomfort, whether physical, mental, or both. I invite myself to openly notice what is going on. I like spotting it and naming it. It relieves the tension of the patterned reactivity for me. It is where everything shifts from subtle irritation or displeasure to a more neutral acceptance.

My first ketamine-assisted therapy session was a profound illustration of this. It was all discomfort. I felt intense physical pain and restlessness, convinced I was having a stroke or a heart attack. I was incredibly distracted by my husband and dogs, and I found myself beating myself up, convinced I had somehow completely "fucked up" the experience. In the coming weeks, as I reflected on this session, a profound realization emerged: noticing how much of this discomfort, fear, resistance, and self-judgment was present in my daily life unconsciously. This session, along with the insights from the full 6-part journey, solidified for me that the path is not about escaping discomfort, but about becoming aware of it, even in its most overwhelming forms, and integrating that awareness for liberation.

A Compassionate Perspective: Discomfort and Joy Can Coexist

Although discomfort is part of our lives, this truth is not bleak. Discomfort does not cancel out joy or peace. In fact, both can be present at the same time. In a meditation practice, we cultivate a neutral viewpoint where we can simply observe, noting, "Oh, that is discomfort," and "Oh, that is joy." From this perspective, we begin to see that life is a rich and dynamic flow of experiences, none of which are permanent.

For example, I have found that moments of connection, kindness, and gratitude can arise even during painful or stressful times. These moments may be as subtle as a smile exchanged with a stranger or the quiet sound of rain on a hard day, but they remind us that joy is always present, even amid difficulty. The practice of observing without judgment helps us realize that discomfort and joy are not opposite; they coexist like threads in the same tapestry. Our goal is not to cling to one or push the other away but to sit at the center and bear witness to the whole experience of living.

Practical Exercise: The Foundational Act of Noticing

The journey of Brave Awareness begins with a single, foundational act: *noticing*. This week, your goal is not to change anything, but to build the muscle of your attention. Here is a tangible practice to help you.

Practice: The Mala Bead Anchor

For this practice, find a string of mala beads, a rosary, or even just a handful of small stones to keep in your pocket. Several times a day, take one minute to sit quietly, close your eyes, and relax your body. Each time you notice something, a pain in your back, a passing thought, the sound of a car, a feeling of discomfort, a sensation of warmth, simply move one bead or touch one stone.

Let the entire exercise be about marking the pattern of *noticing*, rather than striving for a "bliss break" or a "bubble bath for the brain." This actively helps you notice a positive experience of repatterning your attention.

The Reflection:

At the end of the day, reflect in a journal on one of the following questions:

- Where did I notice discomfort show up in my body today?
- Was there a moment of joy that arose, even amidst difficulty? What did that feel like?
- What would it have been like to stay grounded for just one more breath during an uncomfortable moment?

This journey of Brave Awareness begins not by changing your circumstances, but by changing your relationship with them. It is a quiet revolution, built on the **simple awareness** of noticing, without judgment, without resistance, and without the need for things to be different. Each moment you choose to turn towards what is, instead of turning away, you are cultivating the very safety and peace you have always sought outside yourself. This is not about eradicating fear or eliminating discomfort; it is about discovering that you are bigger than both. As you move forward, remember that every experience, subtle or profound, is an invitation to deepen your awareness. It is in these thousands of small returns to yourself that true liberation is found, here and now, even when life is not perfect.

Chapter 2: The Hidden Master: How Fear Controls Your Life Without You Knowing

If suffering is everywhere, woven into the fabric of our daily lives, then what is driving it? Why do we resist reality? Why do we grasp fleeting joy and push away discomfort?

The answer is deceptively simple: fear. Fear is the undercurrent of the human experience, the primal force that dictates our thoughts, emotions, and actions. It is what keeps us in cycles of attachment and aversion. We cling to what feels good because we fear losing it. We push away what feels bad because we fear its permanence. We live on high alert, often without realizing it, reacting to the world as if we are under constant threat. As we have seen, fear rarely announces itself directly. Instead, it disguises itself in the subtle undercurrents of our lives, in moments of frustration, a pang of longing, or a flash of irritation. This chapter is about unmasking that hidden master, seeing how it has shaped our lives without us even knowing, and learning to reclaim our agency from its grip.

My Path Through Hidden Fear: Early Lessons in Compliance and Control

I began forming my relationship with fear long before I had the language to understand it. Growing up as a sensitive, artistic, and likely neurodivergent child in a home that valued discipline over emotional understanding, I quickly learned that safety meant compliance, invisibility, or performance. My mother, while loving in her way, parented through intense emotional outbursts, frequent verbal criticism, and sometimes physical punishment.

My creative mind struggled in the rigid structure of traditional education, and subjects like math felt like insurmountable walls. I remember bringing home a report card with a low grade in math, a subject that back then never quite made sense to me. As soon as I handed it over, the interrogation began. Not questions of how I was feeling or how I might be helped, but instead an endless berating. The kitchen table became a courtroom. I sat for hours being questioned, "Why don't you understand this?" "Are you even trying?" I remember shrinking under their anger, struggling to answer a question I did not understand myself. When I said, "I do not know why," the rage intensified. I was told I was lazy, ungrateful, and even stupid. And because I was still a child, I believed it.

This was not just discipline; it was the birth of shame. That experience became a blueprint for how I navigated fear by internalizing it. Believing it was my fault. By striving to be perfect, not because I wanted to excel, but because I wanted the yelling to stop. That seed of fear, of not being enough, took root in those early moments, and I internalized the message that my confusion equaled stupidity, that my difference was a defect.

Over time, I became anxious, perfectionistic, and deeply attuned to the emotional weather of others. I overcompensated in the areas where I could shine through art, creativity, and later, spiritual insight. Looking back, I can see the formation of a fear-based self. I became overly sensitive to tone, deeply afraid of conflict, and constantly scanning others for signs of disapproval. I was not just trying to be loved; I was trying to survive. And that habit was carried out through adulthood. Even today, in my fifties, I can feel that child inside me bracing for rejection when I imagine telling my parents something they will not like. That is the nature of fear when it forms early: it becomes a thread in our nervous system, woven into our sense of self. And unless we learn to see it clearly and meet it with compassion, it continues to direct our lives from behind the curtain.

I have spent much of my life wrestling with anxiety, depression, and the physical manifestation of suffering in the form of migraines. For years, I believed the cause of my discomfort was external, that my suffering came from stress, circumstances, or physical ailments. But it was not until a series of ketamine assisted therapy sessions that I began to see clearly: fear was at the root of it all. Fear of failure. Fear of inadequacy. Fear of being unseen, unheard, and unvalued. These fears had been shaping my choices and reactions long before I was aware of them. They made me avoid conflict, shut down when interrupted, and overextend myself in search of validation. They made me attach to fleeting moments of relief, whether through food, entertainment, or approval from others, because I feared the discomfort of simply being.

The Brave Awareness Solution: Unmasking Fear

And yet, when I finally saw my fears clearly, I realized something astonishing: fear is not the enemy. It is simply a survival mechanism, a deeply conditioned response meant to protect us. But in a world where we are not under constant physical threat, these fears often misfire, keeping us in a cycle of unnecessary suffering.

Brave Awareness does not tiptoe around this truth, nor does it shame it. It looks directly at what is driving the panic and tells the truth. The

Brave Awareness approach specifically equips us to deal with these hidden, pervasive fears by pulling them into the spotlight. It is about recognizing that much of the chaos we are living in, politically, relationally, and internally, is driven by fear that is not being seen clearly. When fear becomes the foundation, control becomes the strategy, division becomes the tool, and cruelty becomes the cost. As we discussed in the last chapter, noticing it into awareness is the first step. We must acknowledge that we are doing it, that we are trapped in a pattern of thoughts and reactions. Once we drag it into consciousness, then it changes. Then I can understand my terribly, shitty reactions, and further, we understand that the other person (or people) behaving badly is also having a patterned reaction, and from that, we can then have an actively compassionate response to the situation. See how simple this is?

Brave Awareness sees what fear cannot. It sees that the danger is no longer immediate. That you are no longer helpless. That you are no longer alone. You do not need to make fear your enemy. You also do not have to let it run your life. You can see it for what it is: A first response. Not a final truth. Brave Awareness says: You are not crazy. You are not broken. You were just scared, and for good reason. But now, you can choose something else. Now, you can breathe. Now, you can be here. And here you are, enough. Here, you are safe.

Interrupting the Pattern

The other night, I felt a familiar pattern coming on. My husband Darren was off work, which I always want to be excited about. But if I am honest, his days off usually mean couch rotting with political commentary or drama shows where someone is getting chased, killed, or betrayed every five minutes. It is not just background noise. For me, it is overstimulating chaos, and it alienates me. I get it; he works brutal hours managing a family entertainment facility, with 10- to 12-hour shifts, often getting home at 2 or 3 a.m. He gives everything until his brain is just fried. And when he is finally home, I can feel like I am losing him to those screens instead of spending real time together. Thursday night, I was making dinner, which is usually the time that we reconnect. We chat, vent, and shift into us mode. But instead, he queued up CNN again. After a little while, I gave a gentle nudge and said, "Is there anything else on?" And he immediately replied, "Yes." But he did not change it. And I muttered something like, "Is there a show where we can watch paint dry instead?" I felt the snarkiness coming on, my classic, passive-aggressive tone. I felt it rising. I felt the resentment, the loneliness, the disappointment, and the sense that I was invisible again. And then no one was listening.

After I lost my patience, I got up and walked toward the kitchen. He asked, "So what shall we watch?" And I snapped, not yelling, but sharp in a sing-songy voice. I said, "Not this!" And I could feel it spiraling. I knew this pattern. It was not about the news or the noise. It was about feeling unseen, ignored. Like, I did not matter in my own home.

And when I caught it, I caught it. "Oh, I am in a pattern." And instead of escalating, I paused, actually walked up the stairs, grabbed my noise-canceling earbuds, and shoved them in my ears, then tapped on my Amazon Music dance party playlist. And Lizzo came to my rescue immediately, singing "It's About Damn Time." And I laughed aloud and said, "Yes, it is!"

I was still a little bit irritated as I danced down the stairs, but now I was doing something different. I noticed the trigger, interrupted the slide, and chose a new response. This is the real work. Not sitting on a cushion waiting for bliss but instead noticing the sharp edge of an old wound and deciding not to cut anyone with it. It is the shift from self-judgment to self-awareness, where we begin to see our patterns as inherited defenses, rather than fatal flaws. That single choice, to interrupt the slide and choose a new response, is the entire practice in a nutshell.

Noticing the Hidden Master

Fear does not always crash into our lives with sirens and panic. More often, it tiptoes in disguised as something else entirely. It might show up as irritation when a driver cuts us off in traffic, but what we are really feeling is not just anger; it is fear: fear of being unseen, fear of being disrespected, fear of losing control in a world that already feels chaotic. We no longer must be dragged by our old stories. Instead, we can pause. We can soften. We can respond from a place of presence, not panic. And that single shift, from reactivity to awareness, is what begins to dissolve the suffering that fear has quietly shaped for so long.

Practical Exercise: A Field Mission to Find Fear

This week, your practice is to become a detective of your own inner world. Your mission is not to analyze or fix fear, but simply to find the hidden fingerprints in your daily life.

Fear rarely announces itself in the mind first; it shows up in the body. Pay close attention to the subtle physical cues: a slight tightening in your chest when a particular name appears on your phone, the shallow breath you take before making a phone call, or the clench in your jaw when you feel misunderstood in a conversation.

When you notice one of these physical signals, your only task is to pause and gently name the fear that might be underneath. Say to yourself, silently and with compassion:

- *"Ah, this is the fear of disapproval."*
- *"This is the fear of getting it wrong."*
- *"This is the fear of being unseen."*

At the end of each day, open your journal and create a simple "Fear Log." Note the moments you caught fear's signal in your body and the name you gave it. Remember, you are not judging the fear or trying to make it go away. You are simply practicing the brave art of seeing it clearly.

Chapter 3: You Are Not Your Mind & Finding the Awareness Behind the Noise

Unconscious distraction is the default state of modern life. It is astonishing how easily we slip into unconscious patterns. We pick up our phones the moment there is a lull in conversation. We scroll on social media while waiting in line, flip on the TV the second we get home, or snack without noticing the taste of the food. In the modern world, distraction is not just available; it is engineered. Our habits of avoidance are so deeply ingrained that we often do not even realize we are doing them. We live in a society that is in perpetual motion, filling every space with noise, screens, and tasks to avoid the discomfort of stillness. But what are we really avoiding? What is underneath our constant craving for stimulation? The answer, often, is that we are avoiding being alone with ourselves and our untamed thought narratives.

The Allure of Distraction

Social media, streaming platforms, news cycles, and online shopping have mastered the art of stealing our attention. Every notification, autoplay feature, and personalized algorithm is designed to hook us and keep us hooked. These platforms are not neutral; they are built to exploit our psychology, to keep us engaged, numb, and craving more. Take social media, for example. The instant gratification of likes and comments taps into our brain's reward system, flooding us with tiny bursts of dopamine. The next time we feel even the slightest discomfort, boredom, loneliness, or uncertainty, we instinctively reach for our phones, craving another hit. But does it actually fulfill us? Most of the time, no. Instead, we find ourselves in a trance, scrolling endlessly, unaware of the minutes (or hours) that have disappeared. We come up for air only to wonder where the day went or why we feel more drained than when we started. Similarly, television shows and movies often revolve around conflict and drama. Consider the Real Housewives franchise on the Bravo Network. These shows, while marketed as entertainment, are carefully curated to highlight arguments, betrayals, and explosive emotional reactions. The result? We watch people in heightened states of conflict, unconsciously normalizing that as a mode of human interaction. We tell ourselves we are just unwinding, but in reality, we are feeding our nervous systems a steady diet of division and dissatisfaction. We are not just distracted; we are conditioned.

The political discourse that grips so much of the world right now has increasingly taken on the energy of a sports rivalry. Instead of engaging in meaningful dialogue, we pick sides, cheer for wins, and celebrate when our opponents lose. We are no longer debating issues; we are defending teams. Those tricky social media algorithms exacerbate this, creating echo chambers where our own narrow views are reinforced and opposing perspectives are demonized. We experience a manufactured sense of righteousness, convinced that those who disagree with us are not just wrong but dangerous. The dynamic fuels constant tension, frustration, and emotional exhaustion. But here is the truth: this is not engagement; it is entrapment.

My Personal Story: A Day in the Life of Distraction

Let me walk you through a recent morning. I have two dogs, Millie, a four-year-old mini dachshund, and Aurora, a seven-year-old paraplegic rescue who's part corgi and part golden retriever. I lovingly call them the GGs, short for "Good Girls." Around 5:30 a.m., I rolled over in bed, and like a line of falling dominoes, their day began the second they sensed I was awake. Aurora began rustling in her bed, while Millie tapped the side of her kennel with her little paw, adding some soft huffs and whimpers for good measure. My husband often works nights and got home around 3 a.m., so I tried to keep things quiet to let him sleep. I lifted Aurora gently into my arms and carried her downstairs, then let Millie out so they could go out for their morning potty routine. After some peeing and the occasional "boops", we came back in, and I helped Aurora into her wheels, her doggie wheelchair, so she could move freely. Then the ritual began: the "doggie dance" for food. They know the routine. I put a scoop in each bowl, and they scarf it down while I start the coffee maker. While the coffee brewed, I headed into the living room and did something that might sound odd: I stripped off all my clothes. Why? Because after losing 90 pounds, I weigh myself each morning, and I do not want a single ounce of clothing to skew the number. Naked weigh-ins are part of my neurotic precision, and oddly, they help me feel grounded. From there, I poured my coffee, congratulated the GGs on full bellies, got dressed again, and sat in my chair in the living room, sipping coffee and preparing to ease into the day. Sometimes, I use that time to read, meditate, or listen to an audiobook. But not yesterday. Yesterday, I felt off, foggy, a little anxious, and had a mild headache. So, I reached for my phone. First stop: Facebook. I like it because it gives me passive updates on people I care about, which is low effort of socializing for introverts. But it did not take long to run into heated political posts, and I just did not have the emotional bandwidth to get pulled into that noise. So, I switched to Instagram. It is more interest-driven and feels less personal. My feed is full of shirtless fitness guys (for "inspiration"), self-help folks like Mel Robbins and Simon Sinek, and a smattering of dog videos. It felt good at first. Comforting. Entertaining. But the scroll did not stop. Two hours. I was scrolling for two hours. At some point, I clicked on a supplement ad, popped over to Amazon, placed an order, and then jumped back into the Instagram feed. Somewhere down the rabbit hole of fit guys and lifestyle advice, I clicked on one guy who had a fitness app. Suddenly, I am on his app page, subscribed and watching content I did not even plan to see. Then I looked up and said aloud, "Oh shit. Where did all that time go?" It was not just the loss of time. It was the realization that I had been trying to soothe something I did not want to feel. The fogginess. The disconnection. The headache. The low hum of self-doubt. But here is what I did differently: I caught it. I did not shame myself. I did not spiral deeper. I did not pretend it did not happen. I simply noticed. And then I shifted. I got up, filled my water bottle, and went downstairs to my meditation and workout space, where I spent the next hour grounding back into my body. Yoga, movement, presence. My husband eventually woke up, and I joined him in the living room before making my second cup of coffee and heading to my office to write. That moment, when I catch myself and gently redirect, is the practice. It is not about being perfect. It is about returning.

The Brave Awareness Solution: Separating Self from Thought

When we are lost in the mind's noise, we tend to claim every thought as our own. For fuck's sake, a thought is just a thought! Just because your brain fires off an image or a narrative does not make it a product that you are now responsible for. We must start seeing thoughts as they are, not damning ourselves for every one of them. Calm is the immediate reward.

For most of our lives, we are living inside the mind's storm, completely unaware that we are not the storm itself. We are so caught in the drama that we do not realize there is a quiet, observing presence that is untouched by it all. This is the difference Brave Awareness makes.

Without it, we are trapped in the unconscious narrative, reacting to old patterns rooted in bias and self-loathing without even knowing it. But Brave Awareness is like turning on a spotlight in a dark room. It does not necessarily make the scary things disappear, but it drags them into consciousness. It reveals that a thought is just a thought, an unconscious reaction, not an ultimate truth. And once you can truly see the pattern, you are no longer at its mercy. Everything changes. This is not about escaping the noise; it is about finding the steady ground beneath it. It is about recognizing that much of the chaos we are living in is driven by fear that is not being seen clearly. When fear becomes the foundation, control becomes the strategy, division becomes the tool, and cruelty becomes the cost.

As we have discussed, noticing is the first step. Once you drag the pattern into consciousness, you can understand your own "shitty reactions." You can also understand that the other person misbehaving is likely caught in their own pattern, which allows for a more compassionate response. Brave Awareness sees what fear cannot: that the danger is no longer immediate, that you are no longer helpless, and that you are not alone. You do not have to make fear your enemy. You can see it for what it is: a first response, not a final truth.

Living Beyond the Mind's Narratives

That moment of catching myself and gently redirecting is the entire practice. The true test happens not on a meditation cushion, but in the raw, unpredictable moments of life, just like that one. It is the shift from being lost in the mind's storm to becoming the one who notices it.

Without this awareness, we are trapped in the unconscious narrative, reacting to old patterns without even knowing it. But Brave Awareness is like turning on a spotlight. It drags the pattern into consciousness and reveals that a thought is just a thought, an unconscious reaction, not an ultimate truth. And once you can truly see the pattern, you are no longer at its mercy. Everything changes.

In that moment with my phone, the freedom came from seeing the critical voice, the low hum of self-doubt, as just another thought passing by. The essence of practice is to meet these moments with awareness rather than reactivity. The exercise that follows is designed to help you build this exact muscle in your own life.

Noticing the Hidden Master

The mind's habit of seeking distraction is one of its most powerful loops. The only way to break the cycle is to notice it with gentle, non-judgmental awareness. The exercise that follows is designed to help you practice just that, turning moments of unconscious scrolling or snacking into opportunities for insight.

Practical Exercise: The "Pause and Inquire" Journal

This week, your practice is a specific journaling technique called "Pause and Inquire." The goal is not to stop the urge to distract, but to become a curious investigator of it, using your own life as the research field.

The Process:

The Pause: When you feel the compulsive urge to reach for a distraction, such as your phone, a snack, or the TV remote, try to pause for just three seconds before acting.

The Action: You do not have to resist the urge. Go ahead and scroll Instagram or eat the cookie but try to do it with a sliver of awareness.

The Inquiry (The Journal): Later that day, open your journal. Create an entry for that moment of distraction. At the top, write down what you did (e.g., *"Scrolled TikTok for 20 minutes"* or *"Ate a handful of chips when I was not hungry"*).

Then, answer these three simple questions with honesty and without judgment:

What was the feeling right BEFORE the urge? (e.g., boredom, loneliness, anxiety, a complex thought I wanted to avoid).

What was I hoping the distraction would GIVE me? (e.g., comfort, a feeling of connection, numbness, a break).

How did I feel AFTER the distraction was over? (e.g., more drained, still empty, guilty, no different).

After a week of this practice, read through your journal. You will have a clear, compassionate map of your own distraction patterns. This map is the first step to choosing a different path.

Chapter 4: The Illusion of Control

How Clinging Creates the Chaos We Try to Avoid

What we hold tightest to is often what holds us back.

Perhaps fear's most convincing disguise is the one we mistake for a virtue: control. It does not announce itself with drama; instead, it seeps quietly into our behaviors, convincing us that it is just rational thought, caution, or care. This chapter explores how that shape-shifting fear convinces us that our safety lies in holding on tighter, when true freedom lies in letting go. But beneath its many disguises, fear always serves the same purpose: to convince us we are not safe. Fear tells us we must do more, manage more, anticipate more. It insists that we must always stay one step ahead or risk collapse. And the voice of fear is convincing. It sounds like maturity, like preparation, like wisdom. But most often, it is just control wearing a clever mask. Control becomes the coping strategy of the anxious, the vigilant, the over-functioning, the sensitive, and the perfectionist. We do not even know we are doing it. We call it responsibility. We call it compassion. We refer to it as spiritual awareness or emotional maturity. But at its core, our grip is fear, profound, enduring, and quietly exhausting.

For most of my life, I did not recognize fear as an undercurrent. I thought I was being realistic. Responsible. I believed in preparedness. In hard work. In showing up. And I did. I showed up in every room, every relationship, every role with the posture of someone who had it together. But beneath that posture was a nervous system in a near-constant state of bracing. I was afraid that I was not good enough. I was worried that I was too much, or not enough, depending on the moment. I was scared of being dismissed, unseen, or unheard. I was afraid that if I let go of control, everything would fall apart. And I was most fearful that no one would be there if it did.

So, I managed it. I organized. I anticipated. I did everything I could to keep things running smoothly at home, at work, in conversation, and in relationships. I made sure the house was clean, the appointments were kept, the pets were cared for, and the fridge was full. I looked ahead, stayed prepared, and avoided surprises. I worked hard not because I wanted praise but because I needed to feel like I was holding things together. The illusion was that I was calm. Grounded. In control. But underneath? I was tired. Anxious. Hollowed out. Fear had taken root so long ago that I could not trace its origin. But I could feel it in my body every single day. The constant striving for control, this invisible labor, promised peace but delivered only exhaustion. It disconnected me from the raw, vibrant reality of the moment, trapping me in a ceaseless performance of capability.

When Control Is Not Enough: My Journey with the Illusion of Mastery

There was a stretch during the early months of the pandemic, amid all the chaos and uncertainty, when I found a deep rhythm. It was a time when the world felt completely out of control, but in my own corner, I discovered a profound sense of agency. I dropped between 50 and 60 pounds in six months. I was tracking everything with precision using an app and program called Noom. I mean everything, every ounce of water, every sip of wine, every gram of protein and fiber. I became meticulous, a living algorithm of calories in and energy out. My discipline was absolute, to the point that it began to irritate those around me. My sister, especially, would suggest I needed a cheat day. A break. A treat. But that is not how I am wired. Cheating does not feel like freedom to me. It feels like loss, like wasting momentum. And honestly, in those six months, I felt terrific. My body was changing, my confidence was rising, and people noticed. The system was working, and I felt a profound sense of mastery. It was proof that if I applied enough discipline, focus, and control, I could shape my reality exactly as I intended. I believed I had found the ultimate cheat code to well-being, a personal fortress against the chaos of the world. Then came the surgery. It was for a torn distal bicep, a physical disruption I had not anticipated, an immediate and blunt reminder that not everything could be controlled. What followed was a long, frustrating period of working with doctors and physical therapists trying to resolve the pain, burning, aching nerve pain that would not go away. They tried multiple medications, each one a shot in the dark. None worked for the pain. But they did manage to put 40 pounds back on me.

When I saw the weight creeping up, relentlessly, despite my physical limitations, I panicked, but I did not spiral. I did what I knew to do, what had worked so perfectly before. I went back to my original plan, copied the same meals, the same meticulous habits, the same level of absolute control that had brought such success. I tried to force my body back into submission, back into alignment with my will. I weighed myself daily, sometimes multiple times, scrutinizing every fluctuation as a personal failure. I doubled down on my efforts, convinced that if I just applied *more* control, the resistance would break.

But this time... nothing. The scale would not move. My body did not respond. It was like speaking a language it no longer understood, or perhaps one it refused to acknowledge. And I was left sitting in this surreal moment where I had all the discipline in the world, every tool, every ounce of willpower, every single data point, but no results. The internal experience was maddening. It felt like being trapped in a room where you know the exit, you have used the exit before, but now the door will not open. You start questioning everything: your body's betrayal, the efficacy of your methods, and your very worth if your best effort was not enough. It is a terrible thing to feel betrayed by your own body. But even worse is the creeping sense that your best, your absolute best, is not enough anymore, that the control you once wielded was a fragile illusion. This was not just physical frustration; it was an existential slap. My entire philosophy of "effort equals outcome" was crumbling under the weight of an uncooperative nervous system.

And that is when I began to understand something deeper. Sometimes, control becomes a cage. The very discipline that once felt like liberation became a new form of suffering; a rigid set of rules that bound me tighter when life refused to bend to my will. I saw how my attempts to master my body, to force it into a specific shape and number, had become another form of grasping, another layer of resistance to what *is*. And when the body stops cooperating, when outward force proves futile, the only real move left... is to listen. Not fighting. Not fixing, just listening, listening to the body, to the subtle wisdom that lives beneath the frantic striving. That listening is where true freedom begins. It was a humbling surrender, recognizing that sometimes the greatest power lies in releasing the illusion of power.

The Gripping We Do not See

It is easy to associate control with something obvious, such as manipulation, rigidity, and micromanagement. However, the control I am referring to is subtler. It is the emotional labor we do in conversations to keep things smooth. We manage the unspoken atmosphere, trying to steer interactions to avoid conflict, to ensure everyone is comfortable, often at our own expense. It is the pressure to appear calm, grounded, or "spiritual" even when we are seething internally, creating an exhausting inner performance. It is the hyper-awareness of how others feel, constantly scanning for their approval or disapproval, and the shapeshifting we do in response, twisting ourselves into pretzels to fit their expectations. It is how we hold our breath before opening a difficult email, bracing for unseen impact. It is how we clean a spotless kitchen compulsively because we feel emotionally disordered inside, seeking external order to soothe internal chaos. It is how we over-explain ourselves, desperate to be understood, to avoid rejection, to control how others perceive us. It is how we spiritualize our avoidance, labeling procrastination as "divine timing" or shutting down as "detachment."

And the cost of all this gripping is massive. It disconnects us from our authentic selves, from our true desires, from the simple, unfiltered reality of the moment. It keeps us from genuine rest, because the mind is always vigilant, always braced for impact. It prevents true intimacy, because we are too busy performing a version of ourselves, we think is acceptable. It fuels quiet resentment, as we silently tally the times, we have abandoned ourselves for the sake of control. It feeds perfectionism, constantly chasing an unattainable ideal. And it keeps our nervous systems in a perpetual state of false urgency, draining our energy and clarity. We try to control ourselves because we are scared. But control does not keep fear away, it keeps us away from our own experience, trapping us in a self-made cage of anxiety and exhaustion.

Learning to Let Go

Letting go of control does not mean surrendering to chaos. It means surrendering to presence. It means letting the moment be what it is without the compulsion to reshape it. It is not passive. It is not lazy. It is not giving up. It is about choosing to meet life as it is, rather than endlessly trying to manage, anticipate, and perfect it. This shift is not conceptual; it is somatic. It lives in the body. For me, it started with micro-moments. The pause before reacting. A breath before speaking. Noticing tension in my jaw, shoulders, and stomach. I began to see how often I was contracting around the fear of being wrong, misunderstood, disliked, or out of control. And slowly, I began to soften. I started experimenting with consciously releasing tension in my body, even if the external situation remained unchanged. That gentle relaxation, a conscious unclenching, became my rebellion against the illusion of control. It was a subtle act of defiance against the conditioned urge to brace, and in that softening, a tiny space of freedom opened.

Rewriting the Script

Fear has a voice. It whispers constant narratives, subtle and insidious: "I am not enough." "I will be abandoned." "If I do not hold this together, it will all fall apart." "If I do not manage everyone's expectations, I will lose their love." "If I rest, I will fall behind." These are not just fleeting thoughts. They are deeply ingrained, body-level beliefs that have been etched into our nervous system over the course of a lifetime of conditioning. And they do not shift because we tell them to do so. They shift through awareness. Through repetition. Through new scripts that meet us with truth and tenderness, allowing the body to feel safe in the present moment rather than bracing for a future threat.

I began to offer myself affirmations, not as a performance or a quick fix, but as a deliberate act of reeducation. I sought words that felt like a balm to my perpetually bracing nervous system: "I am enough, even when I do not produce." "I can rest without losing my place." "I am safe, even when things are uncertain." "I can trust myself to meet what comes." "I am allowed to soften." At first, these words felt foreign, as if I were pretending to believe them. My mind would argue, bringing up old evidence of past failures or current imperfections. However, over time, through consistent and gentle repetition, they became more familiar. I was not trying to force belief, I was trying to build a new relationship with myself, one rooted in self-compassion and inner trust. I was giving my nervous system a new, more accurate language, helping it unlearn decades of fear-driven rigidity.

The Mala of Letting Go

We can apply the Mala Bead Awareness Practice we learned in Chapter 1 here in a more targeted way. Instead of just noticing any sensation, we can use the beads specifically to help us let go of fear. As you move your fingers across the beads, one at a time, with each one, first gently name what is happening in your mind or body: *"That is fear of being misunderstood." "That is fear of not doing enough." "That is fear of being alone."* It is a way to externalize the internal chatter, to see it for what it is, a passing thought, not a permanent truth.

Then, on the next bead, respond gently, as if speaking to a frightened child within yourself: *"I do not need to grip this." "I can trust this moment." "I am held, even now."*

This practice is not about changing the content of the thoughts or forcing them to disappear. It is about staying present with them, compassionately, consistently, courageously, without engaging in the internal battle. Over time, the grip of those fear-driven thoughts loosens. The urgency dissipates, and the mind learns that it does not need to cling so tightly. The beads become a tactile reminder that freedom lies not in control, but in release.

You Were Never Broken

I look back now and see how long I mistook control for safety. How long I believed that my worth was tied to my usefulness, to my ability to manage every detail and predict every outcome. How often did I think that peace had to be earned through relentless striving and self-perfection? But peace is not a prize to be won at the end of a long, arduous struggle. It is practice. A presence. A homecoming.

You do not find peace through control. You remember it through surrender. You do not fix yourself into wholeness. You recognize that you were never broken, just afraid. All the gripping, all the tension, all the vigilance, it was your nervous system trying desperately to protect you from perceived threats, both real and imagined. It did what it knew how to do based on its conditioning. But now, you can choose differently. You can begin to soften. You can start to trust. You can begin to let go. Not all at once. Not perfectly. But steadily, moment by moment.

The illusion of control will always promise safety and certainty. But what it delivers is fatigue, disconnection, and profound loneliness. Because when you are constantly trying to control everything, you cannot truly connect with anything. Real safety comes from presence. From being with what is. Holding yourself through uncertainty instead of running from it. Let this be the moment you unclench. Just a little. Let this be the moment you remember: The ground beneath you is steady. The peace you are seeking is not out there. It is already here. And so are you. Control had once felt like my only defense against physical, emotional, and existential pain. But I know now that softening is not surrender, it is strength. And the hand that used to clench in panic now rests open in trust.

Chapter 5: The 5A Model: Your Compass for Inner Freedom

The Moment the Blueprint Appeared

For years, even decades, I did my very best to hide my anxiety and panic attacks from everyone, including the people closest to me. For me, a panic attack is not a distant, mental event; it is a full-body hijacking that often ambushes me in the most public of places, like a crowded, noisy restaurant. It does not crash in all at once. It builds slowly, a gathering storm. It starts as a subtle restlessness, a feeling that I need to get up, to escape the people I am with.

Then, the physical sensations begin: a tightness in my chest, like a trapped belch or the first warning of heartburn. The desire to bolt becomes overwhelming. My eyes dart around, assessing escape routes to the bathroom. I can feel the wave cresting, and I know if I do not move now, I am going to lose it in the middle of the restaurant.

I hold my breath because I know that the first real gasp for air will be the one that breaks me. I get up and move quickly, praying the bathroom is empty. Once inside a stall, the deluge is swift. I am choking, gagging for air that smells of cheap soap and disinfectants. I heave, doing my damnedest to be silent, mortified that someone might hear me and assume I am just another drunk at the bar. I am desperate to keep my anonymity, terrified that someone will wait outside to see who was so fucked up so that they can report back to their friends at the table.

The eruption is quick, a minute or two, and then it is over. I blow my nose, regain my breath, and check the mirror to make sure there are no obvious signs of the struggle. No tears, no sweat, no trace. Then, I walk back to the table and hope no one notices. Sometimes, they do. "Your eyes are red," someone might say, and I will quickly lie that I had a "sneezy fit." But the shame lingers, and I spend the rest of the night vowing that next time, I will leave early, before it gets there.

I hid this for so long because I grew up in an environment where if you were sick or something was going on with your health or mental state, it meant something was wrong with you. I can hear my parents' voices in my head right now saying, "What the hell is wrong with you?" and if I could mutter out an actual answer, it was "I do not know," which always led to more berating, more shame.

So, I was doing my best to hide my flaws because I did not understand the "why me" of it all, and therefore did not know much about how to control or manage it. Meditation and putting myself into calm and even serene environments were great, but they did not help much in moments of conflict or uneasiness.

Then, a period of intense personal confinement hit. I suffered an injury to my arm, a distal bicep tear that had to be surgically repaired, and of course, that was at the same time as the pandemic lockdown. My husband, who usually worked ten to twelve-hour days, was now in lockdown with me and always in my space. It was impossible to get away from him. I love to walk outside, and on most nice days I am out for a nice long walk, which helps to clear my head and calm me down. I visit with all the bunnies, squirrels, and birds on my walk with joyful abandon. But with my injury, I was not walking as much, and my panic attacks became quite visible to my husband, who asked, "What the hell is wrong with you?" Of course, I could articulate a little bit more about what I was experiencing, but my attacks do not always correlate with something that is happening in the present moment; it could be a narrative in my thoughts from 20 years ago that is setting off the chain of events. So, I knew I needed to do something and engaged with a few therapists, but again, not everything was about something specific, so talk therapy did not feel like the right solution, and I had enough experience with medications that I knew it was not going to be my answer either.

Around five years earlier, I had met this fascinating woman, Kelly Sosan Bearer, at the Buddhist Geeks Conference in Boulder, Colorado, and I had been following her professional life as a therapist and hypnotist. I had joined her email list and had seen several online offerings for hypnosis-based therapies, and I participated in one great online workshop. Fast forward, I had been doing some research on using edible THC in microdose form to help mitigate the anxiety, and from there, saw that psilocybin and Ketamine were also being used for these purposes. Then came an email from Kelly introducing a ketamine psychotherapy offering that she was doing, and I booked a call. Kelly was someone that I was not only intrigued by from a spiritual and professional standpoint, but I also trusted her to shoot straight. I got on the call with Kelly and quickly learned that because she was in Colorado and I was in Kansas, she could not facilitate this for me, but she was generous with her time and knowledge about what it was all about, and even offered to help me vet some local options for the ketamine assisted sessions.

What I learned next was that there were local options, but they were a bit pricey, and nothing would be covered by insurance. Then the algorithm gods shone down on me, and I started getting hit with ads about other ketamine assisted programs, and I landed on one with a super informative website, and the pricing looked affordable. It was more of a remote program that was peer monitored, so my husband was elected as the peer monitor in my case. I had a few virtual appointments over Zoom (perfect for pandemic times) and was informed that I would receive the first session dose and some equipment and tools for the sessions via FedEx. We set the date for the initial session. Over Zoom, we met with our guide, and he walked us through a number of things. He gave Darren explicit instructions on how to be the peer monitor and how he was supposed to check on me. What to do in case of emergency, etc. Suffice it to say that I was both nervous and excited. Probably more nervous than excited.

I began my session. The medication came as sublingual lozenges that were inserted between my lip and gums and held for 7 minutes without swallowing, while I began listening to some guided instructions on an app played through some earbuds. After 7 minutes, I spit everything out into a cup on my bedside, slipped on an eye mask, and lay back, already feeling the effects of the drug taking hold. The soundtrack and instructions I listened to were good, soothing to me, and I tried to just focus on the mantra of "Trust, let go, and be open." The first session was not a great experience for me. First off, I was fearful and paranoid that I was having a heart attack, and I kept thinking that Darren was going to be forced to explain to my family, who knew nothing about this, how I died during the pandemic in my bed in a k-hole. Humorous but true. Secondly, my body felt terrible and heavy, and I felt like I was turning into a pool of something awful. Third was my husband, who kept coming in quite loudly to check on me. He still has no idea how very loud a presence he is in my world. He even let the dogs in to check on me, and they jumped up and were trying to play with me. Super disruptive! Further, I kept thinking how much money I had wasted on this because it clearly was not going to work, and that I was expertly fucking this up. Smartly, you are encouraged to write a journal directly after the session and for the next several weeks before the next session. I also had a session with the guide who helped me to unpack my experience and met with the clinician who also increased the following doses to get me to where I should be during the session. Suffice it to say that the following sessions were more relaxing, but what I learned from the first was that so many of my discomforts were exposed to me. In recovery, I think that the first step is admitting that you have a problem; for me, it was seeing and admitting that I had been suffering.

After an appointment with my guide to unpack my experience and the clinician to adjust the dosage, the subsequent sessions were a much better experience, filled with profound insights that began to organize decades of my existing meditation practice and spiritual understanding into a cohesive framework. It was during these sessions that I heard a

Ngondro, written by Lama Surya Das, read in my own voice and the voices of my dharma family, Robert, Timo, Yeshe, and Leslie, as we had practiced together reading this aloud many times. This added an immeasurable layer of personal meaning and validation. As I focused on the teachings and allowed the experience to unfold, I began to perceive a clear, actionable pathway for moving through suffering. Over several months following the ketamine sessions, I would often return to the journal entries and notes to keep the experience fresh as I actively engaged with the idea of noticing, affirmation, resolution, and the wisdom that was flowing through my mind. While sharing these experiences with a friend over lunch, it was clear to me that I recognized there was a repeatable rhythm to this process that I could also share with others. It was when I was working with some notes and studying the chakras that it dawned on me that my ketamine sessions followed the same pattern as the chakras. This was a powerful model. From there, and some refinement, we have the 5 A's. While the original 6+1 insights that match the chakras might seem powerful, the 5 A's were a simplified and repeatable format that would resonate with anyone, spiritual or not. This was the birth of the 5A Model.

The 5A Model: Your Compass for Inner Freedom

The 5A Model provides a straightforward, step-by-step process to move from unconscious reaction to intentional living. It is a compass that guides you through the turbulent waters of emotional loops, mental spirals, and moments of reactivity, offering a way to shift out of suffering without bypassing what is real. This model emerged not from abstract theory, but from lived experience and profound personal revelations. It is built upon five key stages:

1. **Awareness** - Catch the Pattern
2. **Acknowledgment** - Name What You See
3. **Acceptance** - Release Resistance
4. **Action** - Choose a Conscious Response
5. **Authenticity** - Live with Freedom and Presence

Each step builds upon the last, training the mind to shift from reactivity to awareness, from attachment to release. Let us explore each one.

Step 1: Awareness – Catch the Pattern

Before anything can change, you must see it. This is the moment where you "catch" the automatic reaction before it sweeps you away.

- **Example:** You are on the checkout line at the grocery store. The person in front of you is moving unbearably slowly. You can feel the irritation rising. Your jaw tenses, your foot taps impatiently. This is the hook. The moment you notice it; you have a choice. Instead of unconsciously fuming, pause. Take a deep breath. Notice the exact moment your mind starts spiraling. You have caught it. This is Awareness. This is the first step in disrupting old patterns.

Step 2: Acknowledgment – Name What You See

If Awareness is the moment when you first see the wave, Acknowledgment is naming it for what it is: a wave. Once you've caught the pattern, your next step is to name it without judgment.

- **Example:** Instead of "Ugh, I have no patience," try: "This is frustration." "I feel irritated because I am rushing." "I notice my mind wanting control." By naming the experience, you separate yourself from it. You are not the frustration. You are not the impatience. You are the one who notices it. And in that small shift, something opens, a bit of space between you and the experience of your suffering.

Step 3: Acceptance – Release Resistance

If Acknowledgment is naming the wave, Acceptance is the moment you stop bracing against it and let your body float. This is the release, the step where we stop fighting what is. The step where we stop fighting what is. Most of our suffering does not come from the feeling itself; it comes from our resistance to it. We feel anxious and then panic about feeling anxious. We feel anger and then shame ourselves for feeling it. But what if you could simply let the feeling be while observing it without judgment?

- **Example:** Instead of clenching against your irritation in the grocery store, try softening into it: "It is okay that I feel impatient." "I do not need to push this feeling away." "This moment is just this moment." This is where suffering dissolves. The moment you stop resisting, the emotion passes like a wave. Acceptance does not mean you enjoy discomfort; it means you stop tightening around it.

Step 4: Action – Choose a Conscious Response

Once you have caught, named, and released the emotion, you can act from clarity rather than reactivity.

- **Example:** Instead of sighing loudly at the slow-moving person ahead of you, you choose a different response. You relax your shoulders instead of tensing. You take a deep breath instead of stewing in irritation. Maybe you even smile and acknowledge, "Wow, I am usually so impatient, what a great moment to practice slowing down." This is what changes everything. Instead of being controlled by your emotions, you become the one steering.

Step 5: Authenticity – Live with Freedom and Presence

If Acceptance is letting your body float, Authenticity, or Allowing, is learning to trust the ocean. The final step is integration, where the practice moves beyond moments and becomes a way of being. When you consistently catch and release your patterns, you start to experience life with less struggle and more presence.

- You no longer get trapped in spirals of overthinking.
- You stop mistaking emotions for permanent realities.
- You respond to life with wisdom instead of reactivity.

This is where freedom begins, not in eliminating fear, discomfort, or suffering, but in seeing through them and choosing a new way forward.

Final Reflection: The Art of Letting Go

At the heart of all suffering is attachment. We grip onto expectations, emotions, and identities as if they are permanent. But nothing is permanent, not our thoughts, our emotions, or our suffering.

So, the next time you feel hooked, remember: Catch it. Name it. Release it. You are not your reactions. You are the one watching them. And from that space, everything can change.

An Invitation to the Path

You now hold the compass. The 5A Model is not a philosophy to be memorized, but a path to be walked. In the chapters ahead, we will take a deep dive into each of these five crucial steps: Awareness, Acknowledgment, Acceptance, Action, and Authenticity.

We will explore their subtleties, their challenges, and their profound power to transform your daily life. For now, simply let this framework settle in. The journey into the heart of the practice begins in the very

next chapter.

Chapter 6: Breaking the Cycle – Applying the 5A Model to Daily Life

The Reality of Unconscious Patterns

You wake up late, already behind schedule. You check your phone before getting out of bed, scrolling through emails that make your stomach tighten. A wave of stress hits you before your feet even touch the floor. At breakfast, you absentmindedly eat while doom-scrolling social media. A post triggers irritation, someone's opinion grates on you. Your mind spirals, rehearsing arguments you will never have. At work, a coworker takes credit for something you contributed. You feel dismissed, but instead of addressing it, you stuff the irritation down, letting it simmer beneath the surface. On the drive home, you replay a conversation from three days ago, something someone said that rubbed you the wrong way. It still has a hold on you, feeding a cycle of resentment. Later that night, exhaustion sets in. You reach for Netflix, pour a glass of wine, and tell yourself you just need to unwind. But as the hours slip away, a familiar emptiness creeps in, the sense that another day has passed in reactive autopilot.

Does this sound familiar?

These patterns are not who you are. They are unconscious loops, habitual ways of reacting that we rarely stop to examine. They are the unseen currents that pull us off course, the silent drivers of our stress, our discontent, and our fatigue. We do not question them because they feel like normal parts of life. We believe our irritation is justified by traffic, our anxiety by our to-do list, our exhaustion by our workload. But what if these visible symptoms are merely the surface ripples of a deeper, unexamined pattern of reactivity that we carry within us? What if the real work is not in solving the external problem, but in disrupting the internal loop that keeps us stuck in repetitive cycles of suffering? This is where the 5A Model becomes real, not just a theory, but a living compass for navigating the ceaseless motion of the mind.

My Struggle: Anxiety, Depression, and the Search for Soothe

For me, food has been a long-time soother. When I am feeling anxious or depressed, I am in the kitchen looking for something to ease my feelings. When I am happy, I celebrate with something as well. This cycle of emotional eating became an automatic loop, a silent partner in my emotional landscape. I can vividly recall reheating a bowl of cold spaghetti but needing to fill the two minutes while the microwave worked, so I'd gnaw on a piece of cold fried chicken. When the pasta did not prove to be enough to satisfy me, I would make a piece of cheesy garlic toast. If that did not do it, I would have a bowl of cereal or a package of Pop-Tarts. This would often roll into a full binge, followed by the familiar wave of shame and self-loathing. The satisfaction was always fleeting, but the dissatisfaction was even more profound.

This pattern did not originate in the kitchen. Looking back, its roots go back to my late teens. When I was about 19, still living at home, I first noticed the undercurrent of depression. I knew I was gay and was unsure what to do. I strongly suspected that accepting my true self would lead to rejection and ridicule from my family. Living on an Air Force base near Omaha, Nebraska, in the late eighties, I was terrified that my secret could cause trouble for my military father. This created a constant inner battle: the joy of accepting my feelings versus the fear that I was a burden on my family. That struggle led to deep emotional exhaustion.

I tried to solve it with external solutions. After a period of sleeping all day to avoid the world, my mother gently suggested I see a doctor. He was helpful, prescribing medication that leveled me out, but also came with a horribly pasty and dry mouth. During a job interview, I was so horrified by the side effect that I stopped the meds immediately. It was a temporary fix, but it hinted at a deeper truth: the real shift had to be internal.

It is only in the last few years that I have found that internal solution. Now, when I find myself staring into the open fridge, I can recognize that I have been triggered, and I am seeking something soothing. In that pause, I can inquire about what is going on. What am I feeling? Am I mad, glad, sad, hurt, or scared? Am I caught in a familiar narrative that I am not good enough? This active inquiry, born from consistent practice, began to interrupt the old, automatic hunger, opening a new space for conscious choice.

The Brave Awareness Solution: Interrupting the Pattern

Noticing is always the turning point to changing the thought, the behavior, and the action. But right behind that is the affirmation that I am okay. I am just a human experiencing human shit. One huge habit that I have adopted is placing a hand on my chest at the precise moment that I catch the mood, the rumination, or thought, and saying aloud, "I am okay." From there, compassion comes in quickly, and I have this feeling of understanding, empathy, and even gratitude. It is always at this point that I can embrace that the experience is not "mine" or a product of "me" but instead it is more like a weather phenomenon happening in my experience. This allows the storm to pass through, rather than settling in and becoming a permanent fixture.

As you apply this model, the shift from self-judgment to self-awareness begins. You start to see your reactions not as flaws, but as inherited defenses, signals from a nervous system that is trying to protect you. You can finally see the fear behind the pattern as something that is simply misunderstood, not something that is wrong with you.

Brave Awareness in Action

This is the true crucible of practice: taking the insights from the cushion into the raw, unpredictable moments of daily life. Here are two examples of practice in action.

The first is driving, a longtime trigger for me, stemming from a nasty school bus accident in high school. The body remembers, even when the mind tries to forget. On the highway, my whole system is on high alert. When someone cuts me off, my reaction is immediate and physical, a jolt that starts deep in my gut. It is not a thought; it is a full-body clench. My knuckles turn white on the steering wheel, my breath catches high in my chest, and a familiar, tingling numbness floods up the back of my neck and across my scalp. It is the body's memory of shock, a silent alarm that screams DANGER.

Only after that physical surge does the mind's narrative kick in. The shock hardens into anger, creating a story that the other driver's carelessness was a direct attack on my safety. My mind might even start playing a movie of retaliation, a whole script where I chase them down and punch them in the face. (For the record, I have never actually punched anyone in the face.) But here's the difference now: I don't have to follow that reactive patterned script anymore.

Because I have practiced noticing, I can catch that first somatic signal, the clench, the shallow breath. I can feel the adrenaline and recognize it not as an order to act, but as the body's old, protective echo. In that space, I can say to myself, "That just happened, and I am okay. My body is safe right now." I can consciously unclench my hands. I can take a deeper breath. Okay, sometimes I end up singing Taylor Swift's "Shake It Off" to myself, too.

The second example is the barrage of daily political news regarding the subversive state of the current government. I will admit that I actively avoid the "news" and have for over a year, but sometimes stories leak through to my social media feed or through a conversation with my husband or a friend. I can often feel that surge of rage at the injustice and the recklessness of politically motivated actions, and again, the desire to stop these people and punish them rises within me. And yet again, everything shifts when I notice my reactivity and see it clearly. Then my wise and compassionate consciousness takes hold, and I know that meeting fear and anger with fear and anger only perpetuates more of the same; it is a stalemate move. I can see clearly that these players are playing a game through fear and intimidation for their own personal gain. I can then shift into wise action by not lashing out in rage and violence.

Practical Applications and Reflection

The 5A Model truly comes to life when we apply it to the subtle, everyday moments where our patterns are triggered. The following exercise will help you train yourself to notice the small emotional loops that run in the background, giving you the power to interrupt them before they spiral. The work, then, is not to rid ourselves of fear, but to meet it with clarity and compassion. Awareness breaks the cycle of unconscious reaction. The very moment we notice that fear arises, whether as resistance, anger, or control, we reclaim the power to choose how we respond. When we start to recognize these patterns, the shift from self-judgment to self-awareness begins. Instead of blaming ourselves for our reactions, we can understand them as inherited defenses, not flaws, but signals. Fear is not inherently wrong or bad; it is misunderstood. It was designed to protect us, but when left unexamined, it becomes the very thing that holds us back. Fear is the foundation of all suffering, not always in the form of panic, but in subtle patterns that guide our lives. It lives in the grasping toward what we want and the aversion toward what we do not. These expressions of fear, attachment, and avoidance bind us to dissatisfaction, even in the presence of joy.

Here is the real invitation: Do not wait for the perfect meditation cushion moment. Catch the pattern in the kitchen, in the traffic jam, when you are scrolling Instagram instead of doing what you said you would do. You do not need to be fixed. You just need to notice a little sooner, and a little more often. And that is the practice. Noticing is not just the first step. It is practice.

Our minds run loops. They see the familiar, even if it hurts, especially under pressure, especially when we are tired, especially when we have been holding too much. Meditation, real meditation, is not about escaping that loop. It is about training the muscle that notices that we are in it. We go from unconsciousness, where we are lost in the swirl, reacting without realizing, to noticing that flicker of awareness that this is a pattern. We move into compassionate awareness, not shaming it, but seeing it. Then to skillful action, we get to choose differently, not perfectly, but on purpose. And we do it over and over again. That is the truth that we are not telling people. This is the daily retraining. Noticing our patterns faster, noticing without judgment, which is the holy grail of this practice. You cannot stop a pattern you cannot see, and you cannot heal what you keep shaming. But when we start to notice, even mid-pattern, we begin to unlock compassionate understanding. And with compassion, we start to see not just our own patterns, but everyone else's too. That is where wisdom lives. This embodied understanding is the quiet superpower that transforms daily life, allowing us to meet every challenge, every trigger, every moment of discomfort with a new kind of presence and choice. It means that freedom is not an endpoint; it is a continuous practice of showing up for what is real.

Practical Exercise: The "Hand on Heart" Reset

This week, your practice is to give yourself one simple, powerful tool to interrupt any emotional loop as it is happening. We will call it the "Hand on Heart" Reset. It is a somatic practice that brings immediate compassion and presence to moments of unconscious reactivity.

The Practice:

The next time you catch yourself in the middle of a familiar, difficult pattern, whether it is the urge to binge-eat, the spiral of anxious thoughts, or the flash of irritation at a loved one, your mission is to do this one thing:

1. STOP: Pause whatever you are doing, even if it is for just three seconds.

2. TOUCH: Place a hand firmly on your chest, right over your heart. The physical pressure is a powerful anchor that brings your awareness back to your body.

3. SPEAK: Say this phrase aloud (or silently to yourself if you are in public): "This is a human feeling, and I am okay."

That is, it. You are not trying to fix the feeling or solve the problem. You are simply interrupting the unconscious loop with a conscious act of self-compassion. This practice, repeated over time, retrains your nervous system to meet discomfort with kindness instead of reactivity.

Final Reflection

Most of us live unaware of the constant influence of fear. It shapes our thoughts, our actions, and our relationships. But once we see it, really see it, we gain a profound freedom. We realize that fear is not a verdict but a habit. And habits can be changed. Not all fear is rational, but all fear is meaningful. And the more compassion you offer to the parts of you that are afraid, the more whole you become. Awareness is not just noticing; it is befriending. And when fear is no longer the enemy, something remarkable happens: you stop fighting yourself.

Chapter 7: Awareness – Seeing Clearly

The First Time I Truly Saw My Own Mind

I have been meditating in one form or another for over 40 years, studying with teachers and dedicating my life to understanding the nature of the mind. For years, particularly before the pivotal insights of my ketamine journey, my internal landscape was often a dull ache of dissatisfaction, a pervasive feeling of "is this all there is?" I would intellectualize my spiritual journey, believing that understanding concepts was the same as embodying them, only to find the same underlying unease persist.

And yet, even within that familiar landscape, a breakthrough occurred. It was not a dramatic event, but a profound shift in perception that clarified everything. I saw myself like an outsider looking in. I could observe my thoughts like a machine playing out its learned reactions. And I realized, none of it was personal. It was just patterns. Fear was a pattern. Resistance was a pattern. Self-doubt was a pattern. For the first time in my life, I was not just *experiencing* my thoughts; I was *watching* them. I was not lost inside my emotions; I was *noticing* them.

This was the profound realization: awareness itself is separate from the mind. Most of us think we are our thoughts. But who is the one who is noticing them? Who is the one aware of the fear? The one recognizing the resistance? That is the real you. This awareness is not a philosophy; it is the direct, felt experience of who you are beyond the mind's incessant chatter. It is the steady ground beneath every emotional storm, the vast, open sky in which all your experiences, like passing weather systems, arise and dissolve.

Most of us think we are the weather, the anger, the sadness, the joy. We are so caught in the storm that we do not realize we are also the sky that holds it all with a vast, unchanging presence. After this insight, the practice of "seeing clearly" became my lifeline. In moments of irritation, I would catch the thought, "They are not listening!" and then, instead of spiraling, I would feel a subtle shift as I reminded myself, "This is just a thought. This is the weather passing through." Suffering truly began to lose its grip, not because the irritation vanished, but because *I* was no longer identified with it. I was the sky, not the weather. This was not about control; it was about presence. It was about recognizing that the "me" caught in the loop was just one layer, and the "me" that was aware of the loop was something far more expansive and untouched.

The First True Step of Transformation

If we were to distill all personal growth, spiritual practice, and psychological healing into one essential skill, it would be awareness. Not change. Not control. Not even healing, because you cannot heal what you do not see. Awareness is the foundation of everything. It is the first key that unlocks the door to transformation. And yet, it is the one thing we instinctively avoid the most. We fill our lives with ceaseless activity, external stimuli, and familiar routines, convinced that staying busy means staying safe. But in this constant motion, we often lose touch with the very core of our being, becoming strangers to our own inner landscape.

Think about it, how often do we truly look at ourselves? We say we want to be happy, but we do not examine what brings us actual joy. We say we are overwhelmed, but we do not investigate what is truly draining us. We say we are stuck in patterns, but we do not trace them back to their origins. Instead, we go through life on autopilot, reacting rather than witnessing. This unconscious living is a subtle, pervasive form of suffering. It is the feeling of walking through a dream, knowing something is off, but never quite waking up. We carry a quiet unease, a constant undercurrent of dissatisfaction that hums beneath our daily routines, a low-grade anxiety that fuels our need for distraction. This is not dramatic; it is the quiet erosion of presence, the slow disconnection from ourselves. And that is where suffering takes root, not in the experiences themselves, but in our complete unawareness of them. But once we develop Brave Awareness, once we dare to truly see, everything begins to change. The act of noticing becomes a sacred disruption, a radical pivot from a life lived on autopilot to one lived with conscious intention.

Why We Struggle to See Ourselves Clearly

If awareness is so powerful, why do we resist it? Because seeing clearly shakes the very foundation of everything we believe about ourselves. Most people would rather stay in familiar suffering, even a painful comfort than face the discomfort of truly seeing things as they are. The mind clings fiercely to its familiar narratives, its established identities, even if those identities are rooted in pain or limitation. This is why we rationalize our actions, justify our reactions, and intellectualize our emotions, all to avoid the raw, unfiltered truth of what is. For example, if you become aware that your job is draining your soul, you might have to change it. If you become aware that your relationship is built on attachment rather than love, you might have to let it go. If you become aware that your anxiety is fueled by your internal narratives, then you lose the ability to blame external circumstances. Awareness forces us to take responsibility. It does not give us the luxury of pretending anymore. And that is terrifying. The fear of seeing is often worse than the seeing itself. We fear what we might uncover, what truths might demand uncomfortable action, or what parts of ourselves might be exposed that we have carefully hidden. We are afraid that if we truly look, we might find ourselves broken beyond repair, or that the effort will be too painful, too exhausting. We convince ourselves that ignorance is bliss, or that staying busy will keep the deeper questions at bay. But here is the profound paradox: when we finally have the courage to look, when we stop running and simply turn towards what is, we realize we are not broken. We are simply conditioned. And anything that is conditioned can be reconditioned. The discomfort of truly seeing is temporary; the freedom it unlocks is lasting. This moment of honest observation is the threshold where transformation truly begins.

How to Develop Brave Awareness

So, how do we build this level of awareness in everyday life? We practice noticing. Noticing is the first disruption in the unconscious loop of suffering. It is the subtle act of waking up within the dream of autopilot, a gentle nudge from the universe reminding us we have a choice.

The Game of Noticing

Start with small, everyday moments. Train your attention to catch the automatic reactions you usually miss. This is not about judgment, but about cultivating a playful curiosity towards your own inner workings.

In conversation: Notice when you are waiting for your turn to speak instead of actually listening. Feel the urge to interrupt but just observe it without acting. See the impulse for what it is, a desire for control or to be heard.

In distraction: Notice when you reach for your phone the moment you feel bored or restless. See the impulse before you act on it, acknowledging the subtle discomfort that stillness brings.

In emotions: Notice when irritation, sadness, or joy arises, without immediately reacting or judging its presence. Just observe it.

You do not have to stop the behaviors, just notice them. Because here is the magic: Noticing alone begins to shift the pattern. It creates a micropause, a tiny window of choice you did not have before, a space where you can breathe before you react.

Catch and Release

I often refer to this practice as Catch and Release. It is a metaphor that makes working with our internal world less about struggle and more about skillful engagement.

Catch the moment you are caught in thought, reaction, or emotion. This is the act of awareness, the split second when you realize you are hooked by a narrative or a feeling.

Release it without attachment, no judgment, no suppression, just letting it be. This is where acceptance lives, where you soften your grip and allow the experience to pass through you. This is not about fixing anything. It is simply about seeing. For example, if you feel anxious and reach for your phone, catch it. Pause. Say to yourself: "Ah, this is the pattern. This is what I do when I feel uncomfortable." Then, release it, meaning, do not judge it. Do not shame yourself. Just see it. You may still choose to pick up your phone, but the simple act of noticing will loosen the grip that habit has over you. Do these enough times, and the pattern will begin to change on its own. It is a gentle yet profound act of self-liberation, releasing the frantic need to control or escape.

Practical Exercise: The Noticing Journal

For the next seven days, commit to keeping a Noticing Journal. This is not a diary about your day, but a log of your inner observations. Each night, take a few minutes to write down three things you noticed about yourself that day:

- A moment when you caught yourself reacting unconsciously.
- A habit or behavior you became aware of in real-time.
- A thought loop or emotional trigger you saw clearly for the first time.

  You do not have to change anything you write. Just observe. This simple practice will retrain your brain to wake up from unconscious patterns, transforming fleeting moments of awareness into a consistent, daily practice of conscious living. It builds the muscle of observation, making you the witness of your life, not just its participant. This journal becomes a mirror, reflecting the subtle ways your mind operates and gives you invaluable data for true transformation.

Final Reflection: You Are Not Your Mind

This is the most important truth of awareness: You are not your thoughts. You are the one noticing them. You are not your emotions. You are the one experiencing them. You are not your reactions. You are the one watching them unfold. Once you realize this, suffering loses its grip. Because no matter how strong the storm is, you are the sky that holds it. You are the vast, open space in which all experience arises and passes. You are not defined by the fleeting contents of your mind; you are the unchanging awareness that perceives them.
This profound realization is the true beginning of freedom. It is the moment you step out of the relentless current of your thoughts and onto the steady riverbank of presence. You no longer have to be swept away by every internal narrative, every fleeting emotion, or every conditioned reaction. You gain agency not by controlling the river, but by understanding your relationship to it. In the next chapter, we take this awareness one step further. Once you can see your patterns, how

do you move from noticing them to facing them with courage? That is

where Acknowledgment begins.

Chapter 8: Acknowledgment – Seeing Through the Illusion and Finding Radical Neutrality

The Hidden Patterns That Run Our Lives

There is a cycle that keeps us stuck. It is subtle. It is automatic. And most of us do not even realize it is happening. We wake up, already tense about the day ahead. We scroll through social media, comparing our lives to someone else's highlight reel. We replay conversations in our minds, what we should have said, and how we were misunderstood. We feel a pang of loneliness, frustration, or exhaustion. Instead of sitting with it, we reach for a distraction. Another email. Another snack. Another episode.

We spend our days reacting to people, to stress, to emotions that surface before we even recognize them. We snap at our loved ones, feel guilty about it, and then numb the guilt with another mindless behavior. This is unconscious suffering. And it has a formula:

1. A Trigger – Something happens. We get criticized, we are ignored, someone offends us, or a wave of doubt crashes in.

2. A Reaction – We tighten. We get defensive. We lash out, withdraw, or spiral into self-doubt.

3. Avoidance – The feeling is too uncomfortable, so we distract ourselves with food, scrolling, overworking, over-explaining, and running from silence.

4. The Loop Begins Again – The unprocessed emotion does not disappear. It just waits for the next trigger.

The worst part? We do not see the pattern. We think this is just who we are. We say: "I have always been anxious." "I just have a short temper." "I cannot help but overthink everything." But none of these things are who we are. They are all programmed reactions, loops that have been running for so long, we mistake them for our identity. This is what acknowledgment is about. It is about interrupting the unconscious cycle and saying: "Wait. What is really happening here?"

My Own Journey: From Self-Scolding to Self-Compassion

It may help to understand that for me, I am in a different world today than I was for most of my life. I grew up in a household of self-scolders who also scolded everyone else. I remember my mother dropping a glass or something and yelling out, "God Damnit Della! What the hell is wrong with you?" Of course, growing up with that, I did it too. For a long, long time. Spilling something and gasping so loudly that it would startle anyone else in earshot, as if a limb had been severed from my body. There was a dramatic and nasty judgment around normal everyday accidents. It feels silly to me now that there was ever a reaction so devastating and self-ridiculing as these things. If others were present for one of these occasions, there would be embarrassment, followed by either awkward silence, people leaving the scene, or even ridicule spewing from one or more of them. "Why are you so clumsy?" "I guess we cannot trust you with anything breakable!" If no one was around, the damage was swiftly hidden from view and likely never acknowledged. This early conditioning taught me that mistakes were not just actions; they were condemnations of my worth, to be shamed or punished.

This ingrained pattern of self-scolding and judgment was something I carried, unknowingly, for decades. I spent much of my life wrestling with anxiety, depression, and physical manifestations of stress like migraines. For years, I believed that my discomfort was external, that my suffering came from circumstances. But it was not until a series of profound experiences, including my ketamine-assisted therapy sessions, that I began to see clearly: fear was at the root of it all, constantly triggering these defensive reactions. Fear of failure. Fear of inadequacy. Fear of being unseen, unheard, and unvalued. These fears had been shaping my choices and reactions long before I was fully aware of them.

And yet, when I finally saw my fears clearly, I realized something astonishing: fear is not the enemy. It is simply a survival mechanism, a deeply conditioned response meant to protect us. But in a world where we are not under constant physical threat, these fears often misfire, keeping us in a cycle of unnecessary suffering.

Today, the response is fundamentally different. If I dropped a coffee cup or knocked something over, I take a moment to consider. Maybe my mind is distracted worrying about something, maybe I was tired, or had worked too hard gardening. Compassion comes in, and I act where I can. Maybe I need to sit down and rest. Maybe I need a nap, or to just put off washing dishes to give myself the needed space. It is not nasty judgment or criticism; it is clean up the spill and move on with care and compassion. This shift is not about eliminating mistakes but about changing my relationship with them.

Why We Resist Acknowledgment

Acknowledgment sounds easy, just see what is happening, right? But the truth is, we avoid acknowledgment because it threatens the entire system. If I acknowledge that my anger is just fear in disguise, then I must sit with my fear. If I acknowledge that my anxiety is a reaction to uncertainty, then I must stop controlling everything. If I acknowledge that my sadness is rooted in loneliness, then I must face my need for connection. It is easier to stay in the loop than to question it. So, we blame others for our reactions. We rationalize our emotional outbursts. We numb out when discomfort creeps in. Because to acknowledge what is really happening means we must change.

The human mind, wired for protection, will tell us a thousand stories to resist this truth. It says that facing our pain will be too much, too overwhelming, that it will consume us. It convinces us that staying in a familiar suffering is safer than stepping into the uncertainty of healing. But avoidance does not remove suffering; it merely buries it. What is buried does not die, it festers, shaping our behaviors and beliefs in ways we do not realize. It manifests as chronic tension in our bodies, as sudden outbursts of anger at loved ones, as a creeping sense of exhaustion and anxiety that no amount of rest can cure.

What Needs to Shift: Reactivity as a Sneeze

We often process our reactivity as if something is inherently broken within us. It is like getting a big whiff of pepper, then subsequently sneezing, and considering that sneeze a personal failure, as if you were not tough enough not to sneeze. It sounds silly, but this is how we treat our emotional reflexes all the time. Our nervous system, shaped by a lifetime of conditioning, is wired to react.

This shift in perspective is the key to liberation. Freedom comes not from stopping the sneeze, but from changing our relationship to it. It begins with acknowledging that your anger is not "just how you are." Your anxiety is not a permanent feature of your brain. These are conditioned patterns, not your personality.

The moment you see this, you reclaim your power. You realize that if it is a pattern, you have the freedom to:

- **Catch it:** Notice the reaction as it arises, without judgment.
- **Acknowledge it:** See the feeling for what it is, a natural reflex.
- **Release it:** Let go of the need to act on it impulsively.

This practice of catching and releasing the reaction is what stops the cycle of self-sabotage and despair. It is the first, most crucial step to moving from a life of unconscious reaction to one of conscious Acknowledgment.

Radical Neutrality: The Space Between Craving and Aversion

This brings us back to the practice of Radical Neutrality, which is the space where suffering ends because we stop resisting reality. Think of it like the surface of a calm lake. The lake can reflect everything, storm clouds, clear blue sky, the passing moon, but the reflections are not the water itself. The water remains undisturbed, simply holding the images without becoming them. That is the open, peaceful state we aim for: no craving, no aversion, just presence.

Radical Neutrality is not indifference or passivity. It is a profound openness to what is, without the compulsion to change it. It means experiencing both joy and sorrow without clinging to either, seeing clearly that all things rise and fall. This is where liberation begins, not in controlling life, but in releasing the illusion that we need to.

Practical Exercise: A Field Mission in Labeling

This week, your practice is a core mindfulness technique called Labeling. Your mission is not to change your feelings, but to acknowledge them with a simple, neutral name the moment they arise. This act creates a space between you and the emotion, preventing you from getting lost in the story.

The Practice:

As you go about your week, your only task is to catch an emotional reaction in real-time and give it a one-word label. Silently say to yourself:

- When your mind jumps to a negative conclusion after a text message: "Storytelling."
- When you drop your keys and feel a flash of self-criticism: "Judging."
- When you scroll on social media and feel a pang of envy: "Comparing."
- When you feel the urge to numb out with a distraction: "Avoiding."
- When you feel a wave of sadness or loneliness: "Feeling."

The goal is to be radically neutral and straightforward. You are not saying, "I am a judgmental person." You are simply acknowledging, "Ah, there is the pattern of judging." This practice, repeated over time, will train you to view your internal states as transient events, rather than as a defining aspect of your identity.

Final Reflection: The Doorway to Change

Acknowledgment is not self-blame. It is self-awareness. It is not about judging yourself. It is about seeing clearly. The moment you acknowledge your unconscious patterns, you gain power over them. And when you break free from reactivity, you reclaim your life.

Moving Forward

In the next chapter, we explore affirmation, how to shift the way we relate to these emotions, turning fear into trust and reactivity into peace. But it all starts here. With the courage to face what is real. With the willingness to say: "I see it now. And because I see it, I can change it."

Chapter 9: Aligning with Truth – Living Without Pretense

The Cost of the Mask

For years, I believed that spiritual growth meant becoming someone new, someone wiser, calmer, more enlightened. I thought that transformation was about refining myself into an ideal version, one that did not get irritated in traffic, did not get anxious before speaking in front of a room, did not carry old wounds into new relationships. But I was wrong. The truth is that transformation is not about becoming someone else. It is about removing what is not you, the layers of performance, the unconscious patterns, the automatic reactions. And what remains underneath is not some perfect, unshakable version of yourself, but the real you. The flawed, human, sometimes messy you. And that person is already enough. That is the real work. Not abandoning the world to sit in a cave. Not withdrawing from society because "no one else gets it." Not using enlightenment as an excuse to be detached and cold. It is about living in the world, fully engaged, but without an illusion. It is about learning to move through life with clarity and compassion, rather than reactivity and fear. But here is the question: How do we do that?

The Burden of the Spiritual Persona: My Story of Isolation

Even preparing to tell you this about myself feels like I am whining or looking for support, like "poor, poor me." That self-judgment is deeply ingrained. However, the truth is that living a life dedicated to spiritual practice, particularly as a teacher, comes with its unique burden of pretense. There is an unspoken expectation that if you guide others toward peace, you must embody it flawlessly. If you teach about overcoming suffering, you must have transcended it entirely. This creates a subtle, insidious pressure to wear a mask, even in moments of vulnerability.

I can feel the presence of who I am when I am teaching or guiding a group. And from this perspective, I have led rooms ranging from 1 to 250 people. It may be apparent at this point in the book that I am passionate about decluttering the landscape of spiritual and meditation pursuits. I want and need to cut away the clutter and make it practical. Most people end up in a room with me because they are seeking something to ease their discomfort. For many, they are experiencing some level of crisis due to loss, attachment, or transition. My goal is to give them quick relief. No long, drawn-out processes of examining their shadows or inspecting their trauma, but some real resolution and relief that is tangible. I have shared this technique with several of my senior students over the years, but my secret is that when I am teaching, I am speaking to a mirror. Every profound teaching that I have shared is me talking to myself. Explaining aloud what I am internally processing. If I led a great meditation and dharma talk about the monkey mind, that likely is what I was experiencing that day as well. This is my failsafe to teach with 100% authenticity. I am not giving you advice that I would not take myself.

The remarkable thing is that quite often the teaching lands for a number of the attendees, and it was typical that I would have a line of people waiting to speak to me afterward to tell me that very thing. "It felt like you were speaking directly to me!" I would hear it time and time again. This is an excellent and validating experience for me as a teacher and guide. And over the years, I became close with a handful of friends who gathered around me. People whom I genuinely loved, admired, and whose company I thoroughly enjoyed. For me, these felt like true friendships that I have wanted so badly for so many years.

However, these friendships often crumbled when I turned to share any of my struggles. It has become clear to me that if the teacher admits they have not transcended the struggles of the average person, then they distance themselves. As I write this, I realize that statement is probably too much to end up in this book, but it is raw and real for me. Even the friends that I have made over the years, who are great practitioners and understand that I am a human and experience usual shit, end up drifting away. It is challenging for me at this point to build trusted friendships because it feels like I will destroy the relationship if I share myself fully. The cost of maintaining that spiritual persona, even subtly, was a profound isolation. It was the pain of being seen for a role, but not for the messy, complex human underneath. This is not just about losing friends; it is about the quiet suffocation of self, the sense that true connection requires a performance you are too exhausted to maintain. The paradox is that the more "enlightened" I appeared, the more isolated I became, trapped in a gilded cage of perceived perfection.

What It Means to Align with Truth Without Being an Asshole

When people first wake up to the ways they have been living out of alignment, saying yes when they meant no, tolerating relationships that drain them, suppressing their real thoughts to avoid conflict, there is often an overcorrection. They mistake honesty for bluntness, authenticity for selfishness, and alignment for arrogance. You have probably met people like this, the ones who suddenly declare that they "just tell it like it is" and use that as an excuse to be inconsiderate. The ones who claim they are "just being real" but are just steamrolling over people. That is not alignment. That is just another form of ego, now dressed up in righteousness instead of repression.

To truly align with the truth means to:

- **Live honestly without cruelty.** Telling the truth does not mean being unkind. You can express yourself without needing to dominate or shame. Your voice can be clear and firm without being sharp or dismissive.

- **Make room for other perspectives.** Just because you see through an illusion does not mean others are ready, or that they are even meant to. Your clarity does not invalidate their experience. True alignment means honoring your truth while respecting the reality of others, even when they live in different illusions.

- **Honor your own transformation without forcing it onto others.** You do not have to become an evangelist of truth. You do not have to correct everyone's perspective or demand they "wake up." You just must live it. Your authentic presence is the most powerful teaching tool you possess.

- **Let your life speak for itself.** The best way to influence others is not by telling them how wrong they are, it is by embodying a way of being that is so steady, so peaceful, so free of drama that they notice something different about you. Your peace becomes an invitation, not a lecture.

When you stop trying to control how others experience life, you stop suffering over things that were never yours to fix. This is not about becoming a spiritual bully; it is about becoming a beacon of authenticity, inviting others into a space of freedom through your own embodied example.

What To Do Instead of What We have Been Doing

Most of us have spent our entire lives operating through reaction, conditioned by old patterns, expectations, and fears. When we recognize that, the next question is: What do we do instead? Here is the shift:

- **Instead of performing, practice presence.** Before you speak, before you act, pause. Feel what is happening in your body, in your breath. Let that moment of presence interrupt the automatic response. This is not about rigid discipline but about creating micro-pauses for conscious choice. It is about remembering that you have agency in the space between stimulus and reaction.

- **Instead of judging,** plant a seed of curiosity. When someone frustrates you, the mind's automatic reaction is judgment. The work of Brave Awareness is to notice that impulse and, instead, choose to wonder: *Why might they see the world this way?* This simple pivot from the certainty of judgment to the openness of curiosity is one of the most powerful practices for dissolving conflict. We will explore this practice and how to release the need to take things personally in depth later in the book.

- **Instead of reacting, respond with intention.** The difference between a reaction and a response is awareness. The reaction is instant, driven by habit. A response is chosen. It comes from clarity, from pause, from wisdom. This is where your power truly resides: the ability to choose alignment over autopilot.

- **Instead of proving yourself, embody your truth.** You do not have to convince anyone that you have changed. You do not have to defend your boundaries. You do not have to make grand announcements about your transformation. Just be it. Let your energy speak louder than words. When you live authentically, your life becomes the teaching, a quiet demonstration of inner freedom.

- **Instead of controlling, allow things to be what they are.** Not everyone will understand you. Not everyone will approve. Some people will still push your buttons. Some will still live in illusions. It is not your job to wake them up. It is your job to live fully awake. This is the ultimate act of self-liberation, freeing yourself from the exhausting task of managing others' perceptions or emotions.

The Power of Radical Neutrality

One of the most liberating realizations on this path is that you do not have to engage in every battle. You do not have to take a stance on every argument, you do not have to have an opinion on every controversy, you do not have to fight to be right. This is the power of living from Radical Neutrality. It is not apathy; it is the profound freedom from being emotionally hijacked by every argument, controversy, or opinion that crosses your path. Radical Neutrality means:

- You stop over-explaining yourself.
- You stop taking things personally.
- You stop needing to fix or correct other people.
- You stop feeding unnecessary drama.

This does not mean you do not care about the world. It means you care about what matters, rather than getting sucked into every emotional storm around you. Radical Neutrality is freedom from craving and attachment to outcomes. It allows you to act with clarity, rather than urgency, with wisdom rather than reactivity. It is the ability to stand in the center of your life, steady and unmoved, even when the world around you is in chaos.

Practical Exercise: The Three-Second Rule

This is a practice I use to create space between reaction and response.

It is a micro-pause, a tiny yet powerful act of reclaiming your agency.

Step 1: When something triggers you , whether it is an email, a

comment, or a conversation, pause.

Step 2: Take a slow breath in, count to three, and exhale. Feel your

feet on the ground, your body in the chair.

Step 3: Ask: What is the most conscious way to respond to this?

If you do not know, wait. You do not have to respond right away. Let

it settle. That one pause can change everything. It is an act of radical

self-governance, reclaiming your attention from the automatic pull of

habit, and choosing wisdom over impulse.

Final Reflection: Live It, Do not Preach It

Alignment is not about telling the world how it should be. It is about

becoming someone who does not need to control, correct, or

condemn. It is about moving through life with peace, clarity, and an

open hand. When you live like that, people notice. Not because you

have convinced them, not because you have forced them to see, but

because there is something about you that feels different. That is how you lead. That is how you awaken others. Not by demanding that they change. But by being so free, so at peace, so completely yourself, they begin to wonder if maybe, just maybe, they could be too.

Chapter 10: What If I Cannot Do This?

Doubt, Resistance, and the Courage to Continue

The Master Illusionist: Doubt as Fear

Doubt is an expert illusionist. It wears the disguise of logic, of caution, and wisdom. It tells us we are simply being rational, that we are protecting ourselves from failure, and that this path, like so many before, will only lead to disappointment. But beneath all its reasoning, doubt is nothing more than fear dressed up as intelligence. It is the subtle, insidious voice that whispers just as you stand on the precipice of real change, urging you to step back into the familiar, even if the familiar is painful. It feels so convincing because it leverages your deepest anxieties and your past disappointments as "proof" that transformation is not possible.

It is not just fear of failure, though. It is something even deeper, something that most of us do not want to admit to ourselves. It is fear that we will try, and nothing will change. Fear that, despite our efforts, we will still feel lost, anxious, and stuck in the same cycles. Fear that this suffering, this restlessness, is just who we are, and that no amount of awareness or mindfulness will ever change it. This fundamental terror of remaining unchanged, of proving our deepest fears of inadequacy true, is the engine behind much of our hesitation.

I know this fear well. I sat in the thick of it, unable to move forward, paralyzed by the thought that maybe all of this, every effort, every insight, every moment of clarity, was just another trick of the mind. I was fooling myself into believing something was shifting when, in reality, I would always come back to the same struggles. I have second-guessed myself more times than I can count, hesitated before taking a step forward, and wondered whether the peace I sought was even possible for someone like me. This is what doubt does. It keeps us standing at the threshold of change, unwilling to trust that there is something on the other side. And yet, here is the truth: doubt does not mean you are incapable of change. It means you are standing at the edge of it, right where transformation truly begins. It is the mind's desperate attempt to keep you in the known, even if the known is suffering.

My Struggle: Frozen in Doubt

My strong tendency to freeze when I am stressed or overwhelmed has been a consistent pattern throughout my life. My first inclination is to sit down and stay completely still. This is why silent retreats and long meditations have been so appealing and achievable for me. Child's pose in yoga is my favorite. I can curl up in a ball with my arms back and feel so safe and calm that I do not want to move or get up. It is a profound comfort, a deep dive into stillness that feels like the ultimate refuge from chaos. This immobility, while outwardly appearing calm, was often an internal paralysis, a coping mechanism to avoid judgment and perceived threats.

In retrospect, a significant part of this tendency has its roots in my upbringing. I grew up in a household where my parents tended to lead with an elevated level of judgment and even irritated anger in the face of others' decisions and actions, including those of their children, even at my current age. My sister has shared with me that my parents tend to treat her like a young kid who needs their permission, even at 50 years old. This pervasive atmosphere of impending judgment created a profound fear of making mistakes, of doing something wrong, of incurring anger or ridicule. Every action felt scrutinized, every choice weighted with the potential for disapproval or worse, disinterest.

So, when faced with decisions or stressful situations, my nervous system learned to choose immobility. Freezing became a learned survival strategy. If I stayed completely still, if I did not act, if I did not voice an opinion, then I could not be judged. I could not be wrong. I could not incur their anger. This created a profound inner conflict: the desire to move forward, to engage, to be myself, battling against the deep-seated fear of external judgment. This is what doubt often does; it paralyzes us, convincing us that the safest option is inaction, even when inaction is its own form of suffering. It felt like I was being suspended, caught between wanting to move and being terrified of the consequences. This inherited pattern of bracing against potential criticism meant that any internal uncertainty could quickly escalate into full-blown paralysis, as the echo of past judgments silenced my present agency.

Why Doubt Feels So Convincing

The mind is a powerful storyteller. It weaves narratives so seamlessly that we do not even realize we are trapped inside them. It takes every past failure, every disappointment, and every moment of uncertainty, and uses them as evidence to build a case against transformation. "This did not work before." "You have tried everything." "You always end up back where you started." "Other people can change, but not you." The problem is not that these thoughts arise; the problem is that they persist. The problem is that we believe them without question, allowing them to dictate our reality.

The mind is risk-averse by nature. Its job is to keep us safe, and safety often means staying in the known, even if the known is suffering. If you have lived in anxiety, self-doubt, or self-criticism for years, then to the mind, those states are familiar. And what is familiar feels safer than the unknown. Even if that unknown is freedom. Doubt convinces us that our suffering is permanent. That we are uniquely stuck. That peace and ease are possible for other people, but not for us. But what if doubt is just a habitual thought pattern, not an ultimate truth? What if it is a conditioned reflex designed to keep us small and "safe," rather than a genuine insight into our limitations? It is the mind's misguided attempt to protect us from perceived future pain by trapping us in familiar past suffering.

The Difference Between the Skeptic and the Scientist

Doubt itself is not inherently bad. In fact, it can serve us if we learn how to collaborate with it instead of letting it control us. I once heard someone say that there are two types of people when it comes to doubt: the skeptic and the scientist. The skeptic looks at doubt and says, "See? I knew this would not work." They take their fear as proof that they should stop trying, that the struggle is not worth it, that change is impossible. The scientist, however, sees doubt and says, "Interesting. Let's investigate." Instead of letting doubt be a dead-end, they treat it like an experiment. They gather information, they evaluate, they observe. When something does not work, they do not abandon the whole process; they adjust and try again.

Which one are you?

For a long time, I was a skeptic. I used doubt as a justification to stop moving forward. If something did not work perfectly the first time, I saw it as evidence that it never would. I convinced myself that failure meant the effort was not worth it. But when I started approaching my practice with curiosity instead of judgment, something shifted. I realized that my skepticism was not proof that I was failing; it was proof that I was on the verge of something new. Instead of assuming I already knew the outcome, I started treating everything, my doubts, my struggles, my resistance, as part of the process. This shift, from expecting perfection to embracing experimentation, began to dismantle the paralyzing power of doubt, transforming a perceived weakness into a source of information.

Doubt, Avoidance, and the Fear of Looking Stupid

One of the most unspoken reasons we hesitate to change is simple: we do not want to look foolish. We hesitate to try meditation because we think we are doing it wrong. We hold back from difficult conversations because we do not want to stumble over our words. We avoid new habits because we are afraid of failing publicly. I have spent so much of my life not doing things simply because I was afraid of how I would look while I learned. The paralyzing fear of embarrassment, of imperfection, of not "getting it right" immediately, kept me trapped in inaction, choosing the known discomfort of stagnation over the perceived risk of public failure.

But here is a hard truth: every single person who is great at something was terrible at it first. Every skilled meditator once wrestled with an unruly mind. Every confident speaker once tripped over their words. Every calm, grounded person you admire once struggled with reactivity and doubt. The difference? They kept going. They did not let doubt stop them. They understood that the discomfort of learning was temporary, while the freedom of proficiency was lasting. I realized something: The only reason doubt wins is because we believe it means stopping. But what if doubt is not a stop sign? What if it is a checkpoint? A moment to pause, inquire, and then choose to proceed, knowing that perfection is not a prerequisite for progress. It is simply the mind's way of testing your commitment to change.

The Choice: Let Go or Get Dragged

There is an old Buddhist teaching that says: "Let go or get dragged". We think clinging to doubt keeps us safe. But it just keeps us stuck. Imagine standing in the ocean, waves rolling toward you. If you brace against the water, dig your heels in, and try to fight the current, what happens? You get knocked over. You get pulled under. The waves drag you along, tumbling you until you do not know which way is up. But if you learn to move with the water instead of against it, something changes. The waves no longer overpower you. They lose their grip. You learn how to navigate them, how to work with the current instead of trying to resist it. That is the difference between getting lost in doubt and learning how to move through it. This is not about passivity; it is about radical responsiveness to what is, rather than futile resistance. It is recognizing that the energy you spend fighting against the inevitable could be used to flow with it, finding ease even in turbulence.

A Practice for Moving Through Doubt

When doubt arises, do not push it away. Instead, meet it with curiosity. Try this:

- **Notice it.** Say to yourself, "Ah, here is doubt." Naming it disarms its power. This act of detached observation immediately creates a space between you and the doubt, preventing it from consuming you.

- **Give it a name.** Is it fear of failure? Fear of disappointment? Fear of looking stupid? By labeling the specific fear, you gain clarity and reduce its formless power.

- **Ask:** "What is this doubt protecting me from?" This inquiry shifts the perspective from self-condemnation to compassionate understanding of the mind's protective mechanism.

- **Thank it.** Yes, really. "Thank you for trying to keep me safe." Acknowledging its intention, even if misguided, softens your internal resistance to its presence.

- **Decide:** "Am I ready to move forward anyway?" This is the moment of agency. You acknowledge the doubt, but you consciously choose whether to let it dictate your next step.

- If the answer is yes, take the next step. If the answer is no that is okay, too. Just do not mistake hesitation for truth. Recognize it as a pause, not a permanent stop.

The shift happens not when you force yourself to believe something new, but when you stop believing the old stories so completely. This practice allows you to acknowledge the presence of doubt without allowing it to dictate your every move. It is a gentle yet firm act of reclaiming your agency and cultivating unwavering self-trust.

Final Thought: Doubt as a Doorway

Doubt will always be there. It does not go away completely. But what if, for the first time, you saw doubt not as a wall, but as a doorway? What if, instead of stopping at the threshold, you walked straight through it? Doubt is not proof that you cannot do this. It is proof that you are already on the verge of doing something new. You are not failing. You are not stuck. You are standing at the threshold. And you, right now, can step through. This is the promise of Brave Awareness: the courage to move forward, not in the absence of fear, but in its profound, liberating presence. It is the moment you realize that even your deepest resistance is an invitation to a deeper truth about your untapped strength.

Chapter 11: When the Path Becomes the Problem

The Pain of Being Unseen

There is a unique and quiet heartbreak that can happen on a spiritual path. It does not come from a dramatic crisis, but from the slow, painful realization that the people and communities you thought were your safe harbor are, in fact, the source of the storm.

We come to these paths seeking connection, clarity, and a deeper sense of belonging. We place our trust in teachers and our hearts in the hands of our fellow practitioners. But what happens when that trust is broken? What happens when the very places that are meant to be a refuge from the ego become arenas for power struggles, inauthenticity, and quiet betrayal?

This is a form of suffering that is rarely spoken of, because it feels like a personal failure. We believe that if we were just more compassionate, more patient, more "spiritual," we could navigate the pain. But sometimes, the most spiritual act is to acknowledge that a situation is broken, and that the only way to protect your peace is to draw a boundary, even if it means walking away. This chapter is about that difficult, necessary, and ultimately liberating journey.

The Spiritual Community Dilemma: My Journey with Hidden Boundaries

Let me be transparent about a period where the illusion of presence and the reality of boundaries collided, even within a spiritual context. This story is deeply personal and illustrates the unique challenges of navigating relationships within a community where expectations of harmony can sometimes lead to self-abandonment.

My journey into leadership within a thriving Buddhist Sangha began years ago. The center existed within a larger spiritual organization and was run by a minister who, I would come to learn, was more interested in power than practice. My predecessor, a woman who had been his right hand for a decade, found herself at a fork in the road between her path and his, and he began pushing her out. In February of that year, she bolted for India, dropping the entire community and its leadership in my lap.

That July, I found myself in the middle of a multi-layered conflict at a retreat with my primary teacher's organization. His girlfriend was trying to run the organization and had failed to pay the facility, which was putting intense pressure on me. At the same time, two of his senior teachers, who saw me as a loyal extension of my predecessor, whom they disliked, directed their vitriol at me. It was overwhelming. At some point, I had had enough. During a retreat, I simply walked out, got on a flight, and left. I sadly have not spoken to my teacher since, and I have honest regret at the way things were left.

Reeling from these two experiences, I immediately felt the weight of my new leadership role and craved support. That fall, I turned to a brilliant Zen teacher who offered to train me as a novice monk and become my mentor. I agreed, diving in full steam. For a time, he was a great support. Meanwhile, a number of the congregation from the old center asked me to continue teaching. Staying true to the Buddhist ideal of teaching when asked, I founded the Kansas City Buddhist Center (KCBC). My new mentor was present for its beginning, and the fact that I was operating a sangha and had earned 501(c)3 status for the organization likely gave him a great deal of credibility. However, I began to feel cracks in the structure. The outward presentation of being a monastic felt jarringly inconsistent with my lived truth as a gay, married man. Then, a chaplaincy internship that had been optional suddenly became a non-negotiable requirement for full ordination. Working shifts in a hospital, comforting the grieving and the dying, was genuinely not "on my bingo card," and I knew the stress would be detrimental to my well-managed anxiety. I declined. It became clear my mentor was promoting other novices with far less experience, just to push me into agreeing. The path with him was wrong, and our relationship ended after a terse conversation.

For five years, I poured my heart into KCBC. But after the pandemic forced us online, we no longer had a strong enough donation base to begin renting space again. I made the sad decision to shut it down. After that, I went through a rainy season of sadness and regret. I had given my talent, my passion, and even my money to these people, these teachers, these organizations, only to be left feeling taken advantage of. I still mourn the friends and the community I built and served. But I now know that their actions reflected their limitations and their power struggles. I cannot take it personally. This journey taught me the profound truth that compassionate boundaries are not about changing others, but about protecting my peace and integrity, even when it means walking a more solitary path.

Stepping Into Awareness: Acknowledging the Wound

After the painful collapse of those spiritual communities, the first step in my healing was to acknowledge the depth of my suffering without spiritualizing it away. It was not just about feeling "unseen"; it was about grieving the loss of friendships I cherished and confronting the anger I felt at being taken advantage of. Before I could extend empathy to others, I had to offer it to myself.

This awareness created a crucial pause, allowing me to see that the power struggles and limitations of others reflected their conditioning, not a verdict on my worth. It shifted the dynamic from a personal wound to a compassionate observation of a painful human experience.

Practical Tools for Navigating Spiritual Disillusionment

The pain that comes from a spiritual community or mentor letting you down is unique. It is not just a social disappointment; it can shake the very foundation of your trust in yourself and your path. The following practices are designed to help you navigate these complex feelings with clarity and self-compassion.

The "Honor the Hurt" Journal Practice

When you feel the sting of disillusionment or betrayal from a person or community you trusted, the spiritual instinct can be to bypass the pain with premature forgiveness. For this practice, resist that urge. Open a journal and permit yourself to write the unedited truth of your hurt. Answer these prompts:

What specific expectation was not met?

What did I lose in this relationship (e.g., trust, a sense of belonging, safety)?

What is the rawest, truest feeling underneath my anger or sadness right now?

The goal here is not to create a grievance story, but to honor the legitimacy of your pain without spiritualizing it away.

Discerning Wisdom from Ego: A Field Mission

In your interactions this week (both internal and external), practice discerning between true wisdom and spiritual ego. True wisdom is quiet, compassionate, and leads to a feeling of inner peace and freedom. Spiritual ego is often loud, rigid, needs to be "right," and creates a feeling of obligation, confusion, or "less than." Notice this in the spiritual content you consume and in your own thoughts. Does a particular teaching make you feel empowered, or does it subtly shame you? This practice rebuilds your trust in your inner compass.

Reclaiming Your Inner Authority

After a spiritual disappointment, it is easy to lose faith in your judgment. This practice is a simple, somatic way to come home to yourself. Sit quietly, place a hand over your heart, and close your eyes. Recall a moment in your life, no matter how small, when you knew your truth, even if no one else agreed. Feel the echo of that certainty in your body. Breathe into it. Remind yourself: "My wisdom is within me. I am my own safe harbor." Do this for one minute every day to rebuild the muscle of self-trust.

Final Reflection: Your Peace is Not a Negotiation

The journey through those painful relationships taught me the most important lesson on presence: true connection begins with listening to ourselves first. It is the raw, undeniable proof of the First Noble Truth: suffering exists. When our hearts are full of the unprocessed grief of disillusionment, we do not have the space to hold anyone else's story.

The complex web of power struggles, loyalties, and misunderstandings that led to those communities dissolving was a masterclass in a second core truth: all things are interconnected and interdependent. My mentor's inexperience, the minister's need for control, the senior teachers' resentments, none of these existed in a vacuum. They were all threads in a shared tapestry and pulling on one unraveled another. And finally, the fact that these friendships and communities, which once felt so solid and permanent, simply faded away, taught me the most liberating truth of all: nothing is permanent. Our urge to correct or "fix" others often comes from a resistance to this truth, a desire to control a narrative that was never ours to write.

By practicing presence, by choosing to honor our own hurt, and by setting compassionate boundaries, we reclaim our peace. We learn that connection is not about having the last word; it is about truly

being there for ourselves first, and then for others, with an open heart
that has made peace with the beautiful, messy, and impermanent
nature of it all.

Chapter 12: Clear Speaking: Communicating Without Abandoning Yourself or Attacking Others

The Fly and the Line

It had been circling for over an hour. First, the kitchen. Then the hallway. Now, here, in the quiet of my writing space, where I'd lit incense, brewed tea, and tried to land gently in the moment, it came again. The low, persistent buzz.

It wasn't just noise. It was an interruption. An agitation that slipped in and out of the silence like static on a clean signal.

I waved it away, softly at first, not even annoyed, just encouraging it elsewhere. The way you might redirect a child playing too loudly near someone sleeping.

But it kept coming. Each time more brazen. Hovering near my head. Landing on my arm. Skimming my lip.

I opened the door to the porch, hoping it would sense the invitation. A breath of fresh air moved through the room. Still, the fly stayed.

I've never liked killing. I've caught spiders in cups and released wasps with a gentle nudge. I believe that life, all life, has its place and that swatting isn't the only way to relate to discomfort.

But then came the moment.

Not anger. Not frustration. Just a shift. The inner stance changed.

I stood up, walked calmly to the drawer, and took out the fly swatter. I didn't brandish it. I didn't chase. I simply held it.

And in that moment, the fly vanished.

Not into another room, not under the table. Gone. As if it had sensed the change, the firmness of presence. The clarity that said: I've allowed. I've waited. But now, this space is not yours to disrupt. There was no longer a tolerance for the dance.

I stood still for a minute, swatter in hand, the silence restored. It wasn't about the fly anymore. It was about the field, the space I inhabit, the energy I protect, the clarity I allow myself to return to without guilt.

I placed the swatter back in the drawer. I sat down. And the writing returned unbothered.

There's power in knowing when to allow and when to end. Not everything needs resistance. But not everything deserves endless accommodation either. The energy of "no" when it comes from deep stillness is a sacred act of return.

The Invisible Erosion of Self: The Cost of Unspoken Truth

There is a particular kind of heartbreak that does not come from crisis, but from continuity, the kind that builds slowly, in the space between the people we love and the versions of ourselves we lose to stay close to them. It shows up in the silence after an argument, when no one says sorry, but everything feels altered. It shows up at dinner, when you smile and nod but feel like you are disappearing bite by bite. It shows up when your heart starts whispering, this is not working, but your habits answer, just try harder. This is the invisible erosion of self that happens when we confuse compassion with compliance.

Some of the most profound suffering in life does not come from tragedy; it comes from the people we love. They are the ones who know our soft spots, the ones whose presence is tangled with our identity, our past, and our hopes. These relationships are layered, beautiful, and often deeply painful. And in the middle of them, we are asked to walk the tightrope between compassion and self-preservation. For years, I believed that to be spiritual, to be mindful, meant that I had to keep showing up, no matter what. That I had to be endlessly patient, endlessly kind, endlessly available. I thought boundaries were for people who could not hack it emotionally. I thought withdrawing meant failure. So, I stayed. I stayed in conversations that left me feeling hollow. I stayed in a dynamic where I was not respected. I stayed because I thought walking away meant I was not evolved enough to handle the discomfort. But here is the truth: compassion without boundaries is not compassion. It is self-abandonment dressed up as virtue. And I learned that not in a moment of wisdom, but in a slow, painful unraveling that revealed just how often I was betraying myself in the name of peace.

The Shift in Us

My marriage has been the most difficult and most illuminating mirror for this lesson. My husband, Darren, is in many ways a good man, but he can also be incredibly inconsiderate and often dismissive of my feelings, wants, and needs. He does not mean harm, at least not consciously, but harm is done. Through indifference. Through casual disregard. Through the quiet erosion of presence.

For a long time, I internalized it. I got angry, sure, but I did not speak. I swallowed the resentment, wore a mask of capability, and convinced myself that I could handle it. That if I just stayed neutral enough, spiritual enough, wise enough, I would not feel the sting of being unseen. But that is not neutrality. That is numbness. That is spiritual bypassing with a serene face. And in that space, after feeling the ache of not being met day after day, I saw something clearly: compassion is not a contract to tolerate mistreatment.

Not long ago, our marriage was in real trouble. The tension was so thick you could feel the air crackle when we entered a room. Huge arguments would erupt from a single misplaced comment and end in the exhausted silence of a battle with no victor.

The shift for me came from watching my parents. They have picked at each other about stupid things for nearly sixty years. My mother finds reasons to criticize my father's every move: the food he chooses, the fork he eats it with. I watch him try to avoid her criticism, but it is like trying to kick a field goal when the goalpost keeps moving. During a visit, an argument erupted over a misplaced plastic box. My usual reaction is to shrink and disappear. But in that moment, to everyone's surprise, I yelled, "STOP IT, BOTH OF YOU! Just stop!"

I retreated to the basement, my heart pounding, and I spent weeks replaying that scene in my head. And in that review, I finally saw it: the ugly reflection of my own learned patterns. I was doing the same thing to Darren. I was criticizing him for the littlest things: the way he set his coffee cup on the couch cushion (just waiting to get spilled), the way he managed our dogs. I was hurt that he was ignoring me, and I was letting that hurt curdle into resentment, picking and picking until there was nothing left but bitterness.

It was one of the biggest and hardest Brave Awareness moments I have ever had. Once I saw it, my first instinct was to beat myself up. But with practice, I started to see that I was just acting out a conditioned pattern, the same way my parents were. And in that moment of clear seeing, I could finally release it.

Over the coming months, I started catching myself in the act. I would be midway through a critical comment about how Darren was brushing one of the dogs, and I'd stop and say, "Thank you for brushing the dogs." Another time, I snapped at him for lowering the blinds over the living room windows. I caught it, walked away to breathe, and came back a few minutes later. "I am sorry for snapping," I said. "I raised the blinds so Millie would not tear them up again." His response was quiet and calm: "Thank you for saying that. I did not know; I was just trying to reduce the glare on the TV." The interactions began to change. The tension eased. And in the space that used to be filled with friction, there was suddenly room for laughter, conversation, and presence. The shift in our relationship did not come from trying to change him; it came from bravely seeing my patterns and choosing to interrupt them with intention and compassion. It saved us.

A Note on Spiritual Bypassing

Spiritual bypassing is the tendency to use spiritual beliefs, practices, or language to avoid dealing with painful feelings, unresolved wounds, or essential developmental tasks. It is a subtle form of self-abandonment dressed up in enlightened language.

The danger of spiritual bypassing is that it creates a disconnect between our spiritual ideals and our messy human reality. It does not heal our wounds; it just covers them with a veneer of peace. It is the voice that says:

- "I shouldn't feel angry; I should be more forgiving." (To avoid the legitimate pain of betrayal).

- "It is all happening for a reason." (To avoid the grief of a painful loss).

- "I am just detaching from the drama." (When in fact, you are shutting down emotionally).

- "I just need to raise my vibration." (To avoid feeling the discomfort of anxiety or insecurity).

Brave Awareness offers the direct antidote. Instead of using spirituality to rise *above* our humanity, we use awareness to go directly *into* it with compassion. We do not bypass our difficult emotions; we befriend them. We learn to be okay even when life is not, without pretending that the pain is not real.

The Brave Awareness Solution: Clear Speaking as Self-Respect

So, what needs to shift? The answer lies in learning to speak from a place of clarity and compassion, rather than reactivity or self-abandonment. This is the Brave Awareness solution for communication: realizing that your reactions are not "you," but are instead patterns.

Before we can speak our truth to others, we must first be honest about our reactivity. As we have explored, an emotional reaction is not a moral failing; it is a natural reflex of a conditioned nervous system. Our goal is not to suppress that initial impulse, but to meet it with enough awareness that we can choose to respond with clarity, rather than being dragged along by the reaction itself.

When we catch the reaction, and we will, then we can immediately let it go without judgment. Shake it off, or wipe it off as needed, and keep going. This is instead of adopting an internal narrative of the trauma, the trigger, the victim, and the impending despair. Your anger is not "just how you are." Your anxiety is not a permanent feature of your brain. Your guilt, shame, and frustration are not your personality; they are patterns. They are automatic responses to a lifetime of conditioning. Acknowledging this is liberation. Because if your suffering is a pattern, that means:

- You can break it.

- You can unlearn it.

- You can respond differently.

And that is the key to freedom. When we live in constant reaction mode, we feel like we have no control over our lives. We feel anxious because we are always on edge, waiting for the next trigger. We feel frustrated because we keep repeating the same conflicts, the same self-sabotage. We feel depressed because deep down, we believe nothing will ever change. But acknowledgment is the first step to regaining control. Because once we see the pattern clearly, we stop being at its mercy. Every time we feel a difficult emotion, we have a choice: React unconsciously (keep repeating the cycle) or pause and acknowledge it. This is the practice of catch and release: Catch the reaction, notice it as it arises. Acknowledge the feeling without judgment. Release the need to act on it impulsively.

Finding Your Voice with Clarity

This is where the rubber meets the road, taking the understanding of awareness and compassion and applying it directly to how we speak and interact. It is about finding your voice, not to dominate or control, but to express your truth from a place of integrity.

For me, this integration has been a slow, steady practice of choosing presence over people-pleasing. When I feel that familiar tightening in my chest, the urge to shrink or to appease, I pause. I remind myself that my voice matters, not because it is loud or always "right," but because it is mine. I practice anchoring myself in my body, feeling my feet on the ground, and taking a breath before I speak. This simple act of grounding allows me to respond from clarity rather than defensiveness or fear.

I have learned to use "I" statements to own my experience without blaming others. Instead of saying, "You always make me feel unheard," I might say, "I feel unheard when I am interrupted." This shifts the focus from accusation to personal truth, opening a space for genuine dialogue instead of immediate defensiveness. It is not about winning an argument; it is about revealing myself.

This practice extends to discerning when to engage and when to step back. Not every battle is mine to fight. Not every comment requires a response. My energy is sacred, and I choose to invest it where it can truly serve clarity and connection, rather than fueling unnecessary drama. This means sometimes choosing silence, not as punishment, but as a boundary. It means letting go of the need to correct others, understanding that their beliefs are often rooted in their own fears and conditioning, just as mine are. This shift allows me to maintain my peace without sacrificing my authenticity.

Speaking Your Truth with Compassion

Clear speaking is an act of self-respect and compassion. It is about honoring your inner landscape while engaging with the world.

The Three-Second Pause for Clarity: This is a micro-practice for mindful communication. When you feel the urge to react, to interrupt, defend, criticize, or withdraw, pause.

- **Step 1:** Pause. Just for a moment. Feel your feet on the ground.

- **Step 2:** Breathe. Take one slow, deep breath. Count to three as you exhale.

- **Step 3:** Ask: "What is the most conscious, compassionate way to respond right now?"
    - Am I speaking from fear or from clarity?
    - Is this about my need to be right, or my desire for connection?
    - Will this serve truth, or just escalate conflict?

If you do not know, wait. You do not have to respond immediately. Let the silence be a space for wisdom to arise. This pause is your superpower, allowing you to choose intention over impulse.

Practice Speaking from Your Center: When you choose to engage, speak your truth using "I" statements. This grounds your communication in your own experience, rather than blaming or accusing.

- **Instead of:** "You always dismiss me." Try: "I feel dismissed when I am interrupted."

- **Instead of:** "You never listen." Try: "I need to feel heard right now."

- **Instead of:** "You are wrong about that." Try: "My perspective is different. I see it this way..."

This shifts the conversation from a battle of wills to an exchange of perspectives, fostering understanding rather than defensiveness.

The Compassionate Boundary Script: If a relationship dynamic is consistently draining or disrespectful, you can assert a boundary with kindness.

- "I have noticed that when [specific behavior happens], I feel [your emotion]. I need [your need] to feel comfortable."

- "I value our connection, and I also need to protect my peace. I will not be able to engage in [specific type of conversation/behavior]."

- "I am going to step away from this conversation for a bit to gather myself. I will check in later."

These are not ultimatums, but clear statements of self-respect.

Final Reflection: The Liberation of Your Voice

When we learn to speak our truth with clarity and compassion, we reclaim our voice, not to dominate, but to truly connect. We stop the invisible erosion of self that comes from silence and compliance. We realize that our peace is not dependent on others' approval or understanding. It is rooted in our integrity. This is the path of Brave

Awareness in communication. It is not easy, but it is deeply, profoundly liberating. When you speak from your center, you invite others to meet you there, or you create the space to move forward with your peace intact. Your voice matters. And when you choose to use it with awareness, everything shifts.

I do not shrink to soothe. I do not over give to earn.

Chapter 13: The Illusion of More – Craving, Connection, and the Lines We Do not Cross

The Subtle Hunger: When Craving Disguises Itself as Connection

Some cravings are obvious. The sugar craving at 10 p.m. The scrolling fix when we feel unsettled. The desire to be seen, liked, and validated. But there are subtler cravings, too, the kind that live in our relationships, where the lines between affection, admiration, longing, and projection get blurred. These cravings masquerade as connection, but often they are rooted in something else entirely: a hunger to fill a space within us that we have not yet learned to hold. This is the illusion of "more", the belief that if we just get a little more intimacy, a little more attention, a little more validation from another, then we will finally feel whole. But this pursuit, driven by an unacknowledged inner void, inevitably leads to disappointment.

My Journey: Navigating Blurred Lines in a Spiritual Friendship

I recently found myself facing this in one of my close friendships. A friend and I had built something steady over time, a quiet, daily rhythm of text messages, encouragement, spiritual practice, and shared progress on our personal goals. He is one of a few students who meet monthly with me at a studio in my home to study Dzogchen and Mahamudra. We also have occasional one-on-one Zoom check-ins where we talk through practice challenges and life obstacles. In many ways, I cherished our connection. It felt grounded. Mutual. Supportive.

And then, something shifted. One day, after sharing a progress photo, a common exchange between us as we both navigate our weight loss and health journeys, he responded with a comment that crossed a line. It was subtle but suggestive, and when I gently neutralized it, the energy between us changed. Our Zoom meeting that day disappeared from my calendar. He rescheduled without acknowledgment. From that point on, his texts became more distant, less frequent, and emotionally flat.

At first, I felt confusion, then disappointment. And finally, I recognized the familiar ache: a relationship quietly dissolving under the weight of unspoken tension. But this time, I did not chase it. I did not try to fix it. I did not ask him to explain himself or reassure me. Instead, I watched. I watched the craving in me to restore harmony. I watched the part of me that wanted to shrink or over-function to maintain the bond. And I also watched the deeper story playing out in him, the all-or-nothing pattern, the tendency to go all-in on something, then suddenly pull away when it stopped feeling controllable or affirming.

The truth is, I believe he had feelings. I suspect he was testing boundaries to see if the friendship could become something more. And when it became clear that I was not going to reciprocate, his investment pulled back. That hurt, not because I wanted more, but because I thought we were meeting in clarity and shared purpose. This is where craving becomes suffering: when the story we tell ourselves about someone else becomes more important than the reality of who they are. When desire shows up in the spiritual community, it can be even trickier. We are vulnerable when we grow. We admire our teachers. We bond over shared awakenings. But if we are not mindful, we start seeking more than teaching, we start reaching for something to possess, to validate us, to fill what feels incomplete. I do not blame him. I do not blame myself. But I do see now how desire disrupts the teaching. And how neutrality, true, anchored, compassionate neutrality, is the only thing that kept me from either collapsing the relationship entirely or falling into the trap of needing to fix it.

Craving always promises more: more intimacy, more attention, more belonging, more meaning. But it rarely delivers without a cost. And that cost is usually the very peace we were hoping the craving would give us. Some connections can be repaired. Others simply drift into a quieter orbit. The deeper practice is learning how to remain whole, either way. This experience reminded me that the most important boundary is the one I hold with myself: to not become someone else's mirror, fantasy, or project. To stay centered in my clarity. To release the need to be understood by everyone. And to let relationships shift without assigning blame or clinging to what once was. In the end, I am still grateful for this friend. For the friendship we did have. For the light he brought. And for the lesson, his distance returned me to: Peace is not found in having more. It is found in needing less. Especially from others. Especially from the stories we tell ourselves. Especially from the illusions of more.

What Now? The Practice of Recalibration

When a relationship shifts or begins to fade, our instinct is to resolve it. We want clarity. We want to restore harmony, to name what is wrong, to feel certainty where something suddenly feels ambiguous. But not every relationship offers that kind of clean narrative. Sometimes it drifts. Sometimes it dissolves without explanation. Sometimes it stays alive in small, awkward touches, polite texts, distant check-ins, but the warmth, the resonance, the ease... is gone.

When my friend pulled back, I noticed all of this. The cadence of our messages changed. His encouragement softened into polite neutrality. The intimacy of shared practice became distant. And while nothing was ever said directly, everything had changed.

In the past, I would have chased resolution. I would have second-guessed myself. I might have apologized for something I did not do, tried to patch up a dynamic that was not broken, but threatened. But this time, I did not. Not because I did not care. I cared deeply. I still do. But because I finally understood that not every fracture needs to be repaired. Some cracks are invitations to pause. To feel. To watch. I watched myself: the impulse to over-function, the urge to smooth it over, the flicker of guilt that wondered if I had done something wrong. I watched how quickly I wanted to solve the discomfort just to feel better. And then... I did not. Instead, I breathed. I waited. I anchored. And in the silence, something new emerged: not closure, not certainty, but clarity.

When Silence Speaks Louder Than Words

There is a unique pain in watching someone you care about retreat from you. Especially when it happens quietly. When there is no argument, no fight, no betrayal. Just space. Just distance. And when the connection had felt emotionally significant or spiritually intimate, the loss felt layered. Personal. Confusing.

But here is the truth: distance *is* a kind of communication. When someone begins to withhold their energy, their attention, their affection, they are telling you something, even if they cannot say it aloud. They are showing you, their edge. Their discomfort. Their fear. Their shame. Or their unmet craving.

The question is not: How do I get them to come back? The question is: How do I hold my center when they do not? For me, this was not just about this one friend. This was about every relationship where I have over-given, over-accommodated, or lost myself in the name of keeping the peace. This was about the wound of being too much, or not enough. About being loved conditionally, only when I was easy, or useful, or affirming. And in the space that my friend's retreat created, I saw all of that. Which is why I did not chase them. Because this time, I did not want to lose myself again just to keep a connection alive that no longer felt mutual.

Choosing Peace Over Performance

There is a moment in every relational rupture when you have to choose: Do I respond from my conditioning or my awareness? The conditioning says: Do something. Fix it. Say the right thing. Salvage the connection. Awareness says: Wait. Listen. Trust what is being shown. And when you respond from awareness, you do not lose your compassion, but you stop making your peace dependent on someone else's participation. This is what I chose. I chose to stop managing my friend's emotional process. I chose not to read into every short text. I chose not to circle back and dig for reasons. I chose to let the silence be what it was, without needing it to mean something about my worth.

What to Do Next: Living the Practice

Now, practically speaking, how do you move forward with someone like this friend? Someone who may still be in your orbit, still texting occasionally, still showing up inconsistently, but with a different tone. How do you stay honest without being hostile? How do you stay compassionate without being complicit in your depletion? It begins with one question: What is the relationship offering now? Not what it once was. Not what you wish it could be. But what is real right now? If the connection feels one-sided, unclear, or unsteady, do not rush to redefine it. Just start interacting with what is true. If you are texting daily but not really connecting, pause and notice that. If there is affection but no depth, presence but no reciprocity, do not force more meaning than what is there.

Relationships naturally evolve. But when they evolve in a way that starts to hurt, we have to ask ourselves: Am I being asked to adapt? Or am I being asked to abandon myself? Here are a few practical ways to work with that space:

1. **Create Emotional Room Without Dramatic Exits:** You do not have to ghost back. You do not have to block, confront, or burn bridges. Simply let the dynamic breathe. If it is meant to

realign, it will. If not, you have already begun the process of detachment without rupture.

2. **Tend to the Ache with Compassion:** Even if you do not want the relationship to return to what it was, it is okay to miss it. It is okay to grieve it. That does not make you weak; it makes you whole. Acknowledge the hurt without rushing to resolve it.

3. **Reaffirm Your Boundaries Without Bitterness:** If your friend sends a message that crosses a line again, however subtle, name it calmly. You can be neutral without being passive. You can be kind without being permissive. Let your clarity become the boundary.

4. **Let Silence Speak, But Do not Make It a Punishment:** Distance is not a weapon. It is a signal. Use it wisely. Step back if needed, not to make a point but to restore your center. Do not engage in emotional withholding to punish. Engage in space to reset.

5. **Welcome the Relationship If It Returns with Integrity:** If your friend circles back with honesty, humility, and openness, meet them with the same. But do not collapse your boundaries to maintain the comfort of a bond that cannot hold your full truth.

Releasing the Craving for Closure

Sometimes, the final stage of healing is letting go of the need to understand. Maybe this friend did have feelings. Maybe they were embarrassed. Maybe they are still wrestling with parts of themselves that have nothing to do with me. But if I wait for them to explain it for me to feel whole, I have missed the deeper teaching. Because the teaching is this: my wholeness is not contingent on anyone else's clarity. And neither is yours.

Chapter 14: The Practice of a Different Truth

The Silent Ledger: When Everything Feels Personal

We all carry within us a silent ledger. It keeps track of the people who showed up, the ones who disappeared, the words that landed like gifts, and the silences that stung like betrayal. When life gets messy, when relationships do not meet our expectations, when communities do not see us, when the world does not give us what we think we need, it is easy to write ourselves into the story as the problem. *Maybe I was not enough. Maybe I should have been someone different.* This way of thinking is so deeply woven into our conditioning that we rarely notice we are doing it. We take things personally because we are trying to feel secure. Our minds are constantly scanning for threat or rejection, trying to answer the anxious question: *Where do I stand? Am I okay?* But what if the path to being okay is not about getting the world to finally validate our ledger? What if it is about putting the ledger down altogether?

My Journey: The Weight of an Unspoken Ledger

For most of my life, I have carried the quiet ache of a son starved for a kind of approval my parents were never able to give. I would share something from my heart, something I was excited about, and the conversation would turn on a dime. The subject would be changed, often to something about my brother, the golden child. I love my brother; he is a great man who has built a wonderful life. Our paths are simply different. But for decades, I interpreted that dismissal through a single, painful lens: I was the lifelong disappointment.

I would get off the phone with my mother and feel the familiar hollowing out, a wave of sadness and resentment that could drain the color from my day. The story my mind told was always the same: *I am not enough.* And I took it personally, because how could I not?

The shift did not come from them changing; it came from the slow, difficult, and profoundly liberating practice of choosing to see a different truth. I began to look at my parents not just as my parents, but as two people who are themselves the product of their conditioning, their un-grieved losses, and their own unmet needs. I started to get curious.

What if my mother's inability to hold my excitement is not a rejection of me, but a reflection of her own discomfort with joy? What if my father's silence is not a judgment, but the only way he knows how to navigate a dynamic that is also painful for him?

This curiosity did not erase the hurt. But it created space around it. It allowed me to see that their actions were not a verdict on my worth, but a signal of their own limitations. I realized that my spiritual practice was not about forcing them to see me, but about me learning to see them, and myself, with a wider, more compassionate lens. This is not the happy conclusion the self-help books promise. My relationship with my parents is still complex. The calls still have the potential to be depleting. The difference is that I no longer hand them the silent ledger and expect them to validate my existence. My peace is no longer contingent on their approval. The rainbow is not that the storm has passed. The rainbow is that I have learned how to find my ground, my okay-ness, even while the rain is still falling. And that is the most profound freedom of all.

The Brave Awareness Solution: The Choice is Awareness

This is the heart of the entire practice. Life is full of complexities we cannot change. People will act from their conditioning. Relationships will be messy. The world will not always give us what we want. The true path to peace is not in trying to fix or control any of this. It is in the radical, liberating realization that you have a choice.

That choice is awareness.

You can choose to be caught in the mind's story, endlessly taking things personally and seeking validation from a world that may never give it. Or you can choose to step back, get curious, and see the bigger picture. You can choose to find your rest and your ease in the simple, unshakable truth that you are the one who gets to decide how you experience your life. This is Radical Neutrality in action. It is the profound peace that comes from no longer needing the world to be different for you to be okay.

Cultivating Curiosity

Cultivating curiosity over judgment is one of the most liberating practices you can undertake. It frees you from the exhausting task of constantly decoding others' behavior for clues about your worth.

1. Pause the Story. Come Back to the Body.

When someone pulls away, disappoints you, or lashes out, your mind will instantly begin filling in the blanks. It will tell you why they did it, what it means about you, and how you need to respond. Before you do anything, pause. Feel your feet. Feel your breath. You are here. The story is optional. Notice the urge to explain, to blame, or to fix. Just notice it. This is where space begins to open.

2. Name the Feeling Without the Spin.

Instead of diving into the storyline (e.g., "They always do this," or "I must not matter to them"), speak directly to the raw experience:

- "I feel hurt."

- "I feel abandoned."

- "I feel confused."

- "I feel rejected."

  This is not weakness. This is strength, the kind of strength that comes from being honest with yourself, without weaponizing that honesty against others or yourself.

3. Ask: What Might They Be Carrying?

This is where curiosity comes in. Not as a way to excuse behavior, but to loosen your grip on judgment. Ask yourself:

- "What pain might they be reacting from?"

- "Is it possible that their response has nothing to do with me?"

- "If I were in their shoes, what might I be feeling or fearing?"

  This is not about figuring them out; it is about releasing the illusion that their actions define your value.

4. Recognize the Mirror.

Often, the traits we most resist in others, avoidance, criticism, inconsistency, are parts of ourselves we have not yet made peace with. Ask:

- "What part of me wants attention right now?"

- "Where have I behaved this way toward myself?"

- "Can I offer understanding to both of us?"

  This practice does not let others off the hook, but it does return your energy to the only place it can truly transform anything: within.

5. Choose the Path of Least Suffering.

You always have a choice: React or respond. Cling or release. Assume the worst or assume neutrality. Ask: "What is the most skillful action I can take right now, not to change them, but to support my peace?" Sometimes that means a conversation. Sometimes it means space. But always, it means moving with awareness.

6. Let Go of the Need to Be Understood.

This one can be brutal. Especially if you value authenticity, connection, and truth. But not everyone is meant to see you clearly. Not everyone can meet you where you are. Remind yourself:

- "My peace does not depend on their clarity."

- "I can let them be who they are without needing them to validate who I am."

  This is the deep work. And it frees you.

7. Create a Ritual for Release.

If someone's words or absence keeps circling in your mind, create a ritual to let them go, not to forget them, but to stop carrying the burden of confusion or resentment.

- Light a candle and write a letter you will not send.

- Say aloud: "I release you from my storyline."

- Visualize them walking away in peace.

    Rituals help anchor your choice to return to center.

8. Reaffirm Your Inner Ground.

When the external world feels shaky, come back to what is always true:

- You are here.

- You are breathing.

- You are more than this moment.

    Place your hand on your heart and repeat:

- "I do not need to know why they did what they did. I only need to remember who I am and meet myself there."

The most compassionate thing you can do for others is to stop making them the source of your suffering. Curiosity gives you space. Space gives you vision. And vision gives you back your freedom.

I release the need to be understood by those committed to misunderstanding.

Chapter 15: The Myth of Control – Letting Go into Real Freedom

The Illusion of Happiness

Let us start with the most seductive illusion of all: the idea that the ultimate goal of life is to be happy. It sounds innocent enough. Uplifting, even. Isn't that what we all want? To feel good, to experience joy, to wake up with lightness in our chest and fall asleep with peace in our heart?

But the moment happiness becomes a destination, it quietly becomes a trap. Because happiness is not permanent, it is a transient emotional state. It is just one of many flavors of human experience, and it does not last, not because we are doing something wrong, but because that is how emotions work. They rise and fall. They come and go. They respond to internal conditions, external triggers, hormones, sleep, weather, memories, even the contents of our lunch or the tone of an email.

Happiness is real. It is beautiful. However, it is not sustainable as a constant state. And when we begin to believe it should be, we start to measure everything in terms of its absence. We begin asking ourselves: *Why am I not happy? What am I doing wrong? What is missing? What do I need to change?* Before long, we are treating normal fluctuations in mood as evidence of failure. We start to believe that neutrality is a problem and sadness is a sickness that must be cured. What was once a desire to feel good becomes a form of emotional self-policing. This cultural obsession with positivity, especially in the wellness and spiritual spaces, has become its own kind of oppression. It tells us that any experience outside of joy is something to be fixed, not felt. This idea finds one of its most seductive expressions in the world of manifestation.

Manifestation and the Cycle of Craving

There is a popular idea circulating in spiritual and self-development circles: that you can manifest the life you want by thinking the right thoughts, visualizing specific outcomes, and aligning your energy with your desires. On the surface, this sounds empowering. Take charge of your life. Attract what you deserve. Ask the universe for what you want and trust that it will deliver.

But beneath that shiny surface is a subtle poison, one that is easy to miss. The modern version of manifestation is often just craving dressed up as a spiritual principle. It teaches us that what we want is out there, just beyond reach, and if we can get the formula right, through enough journaling, visualizing, meditating, or scripting, it will finally arrive. In this mindset, our current lives are never quite enough. We are always waiting for the next thing to validate us. The danger here is not in setting intentions or dreaming big. It is in the unspoken message that peace is only possible once the desire is fulfilled. When we believe this, we turn our suffering into a self-improvement project. We make a desire a performance, and life becomes a game of "if I do this right, I will finally get what I want." And when the outcome does not arrive, the partner, the job, the money, the result is almost always the same: shame, blame, and self-doubt. We begin to think, *maybe I did not align enough. Maybe I did not want it hard enough. Maybe I am not worthy.* The practice of manifestation, when built on a foundation of lack, becomes nothing more than a spiritualized form of consumerism. It encourages us to chase rather than rest, to strive rather than receive, to fix ourselves rather than remember our inherent wholeness. True peace does not come from getting what we want. It comes when we no longer need anything to complete us. Not because we have given up, but because we have awakened to the truth that what we are, right now, is already enough.

The Teabag and the Water: A Teaching on Wholeness

There is a fixation in modern thinking that manifestation is about putting something out to get something back, as if we are separate from the source. But what if we could see the wholeness in both having and not having, in giving and receiving, in movement and stillness?

This came to me in a dream where I was teaching. I invited the students to think of themselves as teabags, allowing themselves to be steeped and saturated by the teachings. But even as I said it, I caught myself. Wasn't I the teabag, and they the water?

The more I sat with it, the more I saw that there is no clear line. The flavor, the depth, the transformation, depends not on one element, but on the relationship between them. It is all one symbiotic process.

This reminded me of a deeper truth about the breath. We often think of breathing in as taking something *into* ourselves and breathing out as releasing something *back* into the world. But what if the universe is breathing into us, and we are breathing back into the universe?

What if it is all one breath with no separation, no fixed boundary between in and out, giver and receiver?

Maybe the struggle of life falls away when we recognize that everything is already part of one vast, complete movement. Like the breath. Like the tea and the water.

Not separate. Just this.

Whole. Complete.

Now.

What Neutrality Really Means

We have spoken about Radical Neutrality, and it is here, in releasing the obsessive pursuit of happiness, that its true power is revealed. It is not an emotional flatline or a consolation prize; it is a form of liberation. It is the middle path between indulgence and avoidance, between clinging and rejection. It is the clear space from which we can observe our experience without immediately identifying with it. Neutrality allows us to feel our emotions fully but not be dragged around by them. It is what gives us the ability to feel joy without fearing its disappearance, to feel sadness without assuming we are broken, and to feel anger without needing to act on it or suppress it. It is not the absence of feeling; it is the presence of clarity. Neutrality arises when we stop demanding that our emotions mean something definitive about who we are. When we stop making our moods into moral judgments. When we begin to realize that we can feel desire without being ruled by it, we can experience discomfort without needing to escape it. From neutrality, we gain the ability to respond instead of reacting. To witness, rather than unravel.

A Personal Reflection: Mad, Glad, Sad, and Scared

Despite what I teach and practice, I still get mad. I still get sad. I still get scared. And I still feel joy, sometimes so deeply it takes my breath away. Emotions continue to rise and fall in me, just like they do in everyone else. But what is changed is how I relate to them.

There are days I find myself wondering if people find me boring or if the reason, I do not have more close friendships is because I seem distant. I worry that I do not match the energy people expect, or that my preference for calmness and stillness is misread as disinterest. I catch myself thinking, *Maybe I am just not enough.* I wonder if life will ever feel more connected, more vibrant than it does in this moment. And sometimes, I question whether I would be okay if it did not.

But here is the difference now: I no longer collapse into those thoughts. I do not build houses in them. I do not assume they are true. They are not the story of who I am, they are passing weather systems in the landscape of my awareness. I let them move through. And when they return, as they always do, I meet them again, this time with less fear.

The Practice of Return

Neutrality is not a mood. It is a muscle. It is something we develop through repeated return, each time we notice the mind wandering, each time we catch ourselves craving, spiraling, or narrating a new fear-based story. It begins with that small flicker of recognition: *Ah, there is that thought again. There is the loop beginning.*

In those moments, I try not to fix anything. I do not fight the thought or try to override it. I breathe. I feel the weight of my body. I place my hand on my heart and say, *I see you.* Not to indulge the emotion but to stay present with it, long enough to let it pass.

Sometimes, the thoughts say, *this is the part where I think I am a disappointment.* Or *this is where I fear I have been forgotten.* Or *this is where I wish someone would tell me I am doing enough.* These thoughts still arise, but I no longer follow them into suffering. I sit beside them with honesty and care. And that sitting, that not reacting, is what loosens their grip.

Calling Out the Illusion of Control

We have been taught, implicitly and explicitly, that the goal of the spiritual path is control. Control of the mind. Mastery of our thoughts. The ability to stay calm in every storm. But this is just another form of striving. Another illusion is that peace is something we have to achieve through force. In reality, control is a mask for fear. The mind does not need to be dominated. It needs to be understood. The goal is not to conquer every thought or manage every emotion; it is to relate to them differently. To realize that we are not our thoughts. We are not our feelings. We are the awareness that holds them.

Our brains are meaning-making machines. They generate thoughts constantly, some helpful, some hurtful, and most habitual. But we are not required to believe every thought we think. We are not required to follow every emotion we feel. They are not facts. They are not fate. They are like birds passing overhead; we do not have to catch them and build nests.

The Real Promise

The promise of this path is not that you'll be "10% happier," or that you'll finally manifest your dream life. It is something more radical. More enduring. More true. It is the ability to stop suffering over things you cannot control. The capacity to see clearly, feel deeply, and live honestly. The end of the exhausting project of fixing yourself. Because you were never broken. You were just caught in a loop. Now, you are waking up. And what you are waking up to is not just clarity. It is freedom. Not the freedom of having everything you want, but the freedom of no longer needing it to be okay. Welcome home.

Chapter 16: Creative Awareness: The Practice of Making Your Own Path

Busting the "I'm Not Creative" Myth

I want to start this chapter by speaking directly to the part of you that might have already decided this isn't for you. I want to talk to the quiet, persistent voice in your head that may have just whispered, *"Oh, I'm not the creative one."*

Where did that story come from?

For many of us, it came from a report card with a bad grade, a well-meaning parent who praised a more "practical" sibling, or a culture that reserves the title of "creative" for a select few painters, musicians, and writers. We were sorted into boxes early on: you're the smart one, you're the athletic one, you're the responsible one. And if you weren't the one who could draw a perfect circle, you learned to believe that a whole part of the human experience was not available to you.

But here is the truth: that voice that tells you you're not creative is just another fear-based thought pattern. It is the fear of not being good enough, the fear of being judged, the fear of looking foolish. It is the same hidden master we've been unmasking throughout this entire book. And today, we are going to meet it with Brave Awareness.

The Creative and the Capable

Growing up, I was the one who had trouble in school. I could read an entire page of a textbook and realize at the end that I hadn't retained a single word. But I loved literature when it was read aloud, and I loved my art class. Give me a stack of construction paper, some crayons, and an old egg carton, and my mind was lost in possibilities. I was the one out of four siblings who sucked in his grades, and I know my parents worried about how I was going to get on in life.

My sensitive nature, my creative spark, and my willingness to play Barbies with the girls in the neighborhood also troubled my folks. I wanted to cook and clean; vacuuming is still a particularly soothing exercise for me. I loved a well-decorated space, beautiful gardens. And I adored music. I sang, played a handful of instruments, and would sit for hours with my headphones on, letting a symphony or a pop song build a world inside my head, feeling every note in my body.

My grandmother, Margie Nadine, was one of my favorite people. She was a movie star to me. I remember her visiting us in New York, getting off the plane decked out from head to toe in red, right down to her luggage and the little wool coat wrapped around her little yorkie. I loved watching the way she moved, how she applied her makeup, and how she did her hair. And she was watching me, too. She saw me. Itching for something to do with my hands, she started teaching me how to crochet when I was seven years old. Holy moly, I was taking some yarn and making something solid from it! I still love it. You can still find me ignoring the movie Darren and I selected on a cold winter night to crochet a hat.

Since I wasn't the "smart" one, I was designated the "creative and sensitive" one. I got into photography, spending countless hours in the darkroom. I was even accepted into the Kansas City Art Institute, but my parents thought it better that I go to a "real school" for a few years first. That was one of the biggest disappointments of my life. But my Gram never gave up on me. She bought me every art book, paintbrush, or art supply my heart desired, and I would lose myself for hours painting, drawing, and sculpting.

But then adulthood came. And like all things, I threw myself into work and, to everyone's surprise, I excelled. I was a banquet manager in a hotel by the time I was 19 and just kept moving up. Along the way, I found out that I was actually smart, that people appreciated not just my work ethic but my creative approaches to problem-solving. And as I climbed, my paints drifted into the closet, then to the basement, and finally into the trash. I still have a stack of paintings that I love, leaning against a concrete wall in my garage, that I just can't let go of. They represent a freedom that pulsed through my veins before it was replaced by an uncanny knack for analytics and strategy.

For years, I suppressed the urges. But creativity always bubbles up. I can see the pattern in hindsight: depression and anxiety would take over, and then, all of a sudden, I would get a spark to redecorate something. I'd rearrange furniture in the middle of the night, creating a beautiful space I felt at home in. The house I was forced to sell was a huge achievement for me; I took a plain little ranch home and made it my own beautiful showplace. Even my spiritual practice found a creative outlet, and I learned to embody the teachings through sound, becoming a guide for others in chant, losing myself in the resonant sound stuff. I still do it. When I feel stressed, the first thing I need to do to get my footing is clean up clutter. I dust and vacuum. I make a trip to Trader Joe's for flowers that I skillfully arrange and place around my house. And then, my brain is calm. I can handle what's next.

I didn't notice this pattern for years. But the very act of writing this book, of sinking into hours of creative flow, just as I am right now, has been its own form of awareness. And in this moment, the final piece just clicked into place.

Holy fuck. I am still creative. And I am ridiculously analytical and strategic, all at the same time. I'm not the creative one *or* the smart one. I am both.

Am I also part unicorn?

My big awakening is that I could be both. What??? That realization—that I didn't have to choose, that my wholeness included all these seemingly contradictory parts, was a homecoming.

We are all multi-faceted gems, reflecting different kinds of light from different angles. For years, I had only been looking at one facet of myself, believing that was the whole story. But the truest expression of Brave Awareness is turning the gem in your own hand and finally, with awe, seeing how all the different parts, the creative, the capable, the messy, the wise, are what make you brilliant.

The Real Work: Getting Out of the Fucking Way

For years, I believed that creativity was something you *did*. You picked up a paintbrush, you rearranged the furniture, you sang a song, you crocheted a hat. And yes, those are all beautiful, tangible acts. But the deeper I've gone into this practice, the more I've realized that true creativity is not an act of doing at all.

It is the practice of **getting out of the fucking way.**

A student of mine once told me a story about how panicked she was while delivering her first child. The midwife calmly held her and said: *Honey, your body is in labor. You have to get out of the way and let it happen.*

That is the entire practice. Creativity is the labor of the soul, and your only job is to get out of its way. It is the courageous work of clearing the path of all the shit that blocks the flow, the doubt, the shame, the echo of a parent's voice telling you who you are or aren't, the fear of not being "good enough."

It is the moment-by-moment choice to **stop stopping** the natural, uninhibited impulse of your own heart. It's not about learning to draw your feelings. It's about seeing your feelings as feelings, seeing your fear as fear, seeing your doubt as doubt, and then stepping aside so that the most beautiful thing, whether it's a word, a color, a sound, or just your own quiet, steady presence, can finally be realized.

This is Radical Neutrality in its most joyful and generative form. It is the freedom that erupts when you stop judging the creative impulse and simply allow it to move through you. It's not about learning to draw your feelings. It's about seeing your feelings as feelings, seeing your fear as fear, seeing your doubt as doubt, and then getting out of their way so that the most beautiful thing, whether it's a word, a color, a sound, or just your own quiet, steady presence, can finally come through.

This isn't about becoming an artist. It's about remembering that your very life is an act of creation. And your only job is to get out of its way and let it happen.

Practical Exercise: A Field Mission in Uninhibited Flow

This week, your practice is not to *create* anything. It is to experience the feeling of uninhibited flow. Your mission is to find one five-minute window each day to engage in a simple, non-goal-oriented activity with the sole intention of getting out of your own way.

The Mission:

Choose one of these simple activities:

- Take a pen and a piece of paper and just make swirls and lines without trying to draw anything.

- Put on a piece of music and let your body move in whatever way it wants, without trying to "dance."

- Hum a single, continuous note for as long as your breath allows.

- Go for a walk with no destination, letting your feet decide where to turn.

The Practice:

As you begin, the inner critic will almost certainly show up. It will tell you you're doing it wrong, that it's pointless, that you look stupid. Your only job is to notice that voice, thank it for trying to protect you, and then gently return your attention to the simple, physical sensation of the activity.

The goal is not to be *good* at it. The goal is to notice the part of you that stops you, and to compassionately get out of its way, just for a moment. At the end of the week, reflect not on what you made, but on what it felt like to experience a single moment of uninhibited flow.

Final Reflection: Your Life is the Art

The most profound shift on this path is the realization that you are not just a person living a life; you are life itself, living through you. The universe is not waiting for you to become a great artist. It is simply waiting for you to get out of the way so that it can express its own beauty through your unique and unrepeatable form.

Your breath, your movements, the way you arrange flowers, the way you comfort a friend, the way you scratch a smiley face into burnt toast, these are not small, insignificant acts. They are all masterpieces of presence.

The ultimate creative act is not to paint a canvas or write a symphony. It is to live your life with such open, brave awareness that your very presence becomes a work of art. You are not just on the path; you *are* the path. You are not just making the art; you *are* the art.

Chapter 17: The Two Wings: Compassion and Wisdom in Action

The Call to Conscious Living: Beyond Theory to Embodied Practice

Awareness is not the destination. It is the doorway. The moment we become aware, truly aware, of what we are thinking, feeling, doing, or avoiding, something profound happens: we get to choose. That is the real power of this path. Not in becoming someone new or reaching a state of perpetual calm, but in reclaiming the simple miracle of conscious choice. For most people, life is lived on autopilot. Emotional reactions drive behavior. Old stories shape new relationships. Fear masquerades as logic. Grief gets tucked into corners and covered with productivity. Craving gets called ambition. Aversion gets called boundaries. We move through our days reacting to life as it comes, without ever pausing to ask: *Is this actually what I want? Is this actually true?*

Awareness is the pause that rewrites the pattern. It does not always come with fanfare. Sometimes, it looks like recognizing that you are irritable because you did not sleep well. It looks like realizing you are about to have a difficult conversation while you are hungry, or that the argument you are having with your partner is really about feeling scared and unseen. It is in those small, unglamorous moments that awareness becomes a sacred act. This is where the rubber meets the road: taking the insights from the cushion into the raw, unpredictable moments of daily life. The subtle hum of unease, the fleeting thought of comparison, the automatic urge to distract, these are the invitations to presence. Without awareness, these moments simply dictate our day, leaving us feeling drained and disconnected. With awareness, they become opportunities to choose alignment, to respond from clarity, and to reclaim our peace.

My Own Journey: The Integration of Inner Truth

There was a season in my life, not all that long ago, when I was clinging to the edge of everything. My identity was crumbling. My sangha had dissolved. Friendships I thought were forever had faded or fractured. The organizations I had given my heart and energy to had closed their doors behind me. I kept asking myself, *Was I wrong to trust? Was I too much? Did I create this?* The spiral of doubt was relentless. It felt like a relentless internal interrogation, each question a fresh wound.

But I was not new to the practice. I had been meditating, teaching, and practicing for decades. And in the quiet moments, especially during that time, I started to notice something subtle but undeniable: The thoughts that were destroying me... were just thoughts. They weren't permanent. They weren't facts. And they weren't me. They were echoes of fear and grief and longing, trying to protect me from the pain of loss. And in that noticing, something shifted. I did not silence the thoughts. I did not override the emotions. I simply stopped believing that they were proof of anything. That is the moment awareness became my companion, not a tool I used in crisis, but a presence I returned to in every moment of uncertainty. This profound realization, born from the wreckage of my external life, became the bedrock of my internal freedom. It was the felt sense of being the sky, vast and untouched, even as the storm raged through. More recently, I noticed it again, in a small, mundane moment. I was scrolling my phone, jumping between messages and apps, feeling that strange sense of aimless urgency. Nothing was actually wrong, but my body was tight, my breath shallow, my mind crowded. I caught myself halfway through opening yet another app and whispered, "Pause." In that pause, I noticed the ache of loneliness underneath the busyness. Not a dramatic loneliness, just a quiet longing to feel connected. I put the phone down. I stepped outside. I watched the clouds. That one breath of awareness did not fix everything. But it changed the trajectory of the moment. And that is the whole point. It is in these thousands of small, conscious returns that the path is truly lived.

The 5A Model in Action: Your Life as the Practice

Throughout this book, we have explored the 5A model: Awareness, Acknowledgment, Acceptance, Action, and Allowing, as a framework for waking up and staying awake. But these aren't just ideas. They are how I live now. They are the practical rhythm of conscious choice, a living compass for navigating the ceaseless motion of the mind and heart.

Let's take an example. Imagine I have had a difficult interaction with someone I care about, maybe it was dismissive, or sharp, or just off. Immediately, the mind starts spinning. *Maybe they are pulling away. Maybe I have done something wrong. Maybe I am not worth sticking with.* It used to be that those thoughts would hijack my nervous system. I would replay the interaction, look for signs, try to predict what would happen next, or worse, abandon myself to avoid abandonment by them. The internal tension would build, a knot in my stomach, a tightness in my jaw, and a racing heart, all signaling the familiar descent into fear-driven reactivity.

Now, I turn to the 5As:

- **Awareness** is catching the narrative early. I notice the initial flicker of unease, the tightening in my chest, the first thought of blame or self-doubt. "I am flooded right now. I am tired and my thoughts are sharp." This is the crucial moment of recognition, the pause before the spiral takes hold.

- **Acknowledgment** is naming the emotion underneath: "I am scared. I am sad. I am angry." It is also saying, "This is the truth of the moment. My nervous system is activated. Nothing's wrong with me." This is where I validate my human experience without judgment, separating the feeling from the story.

- **Acceptance** is saying, "This is here. I do not need to make it go away." "This is not ideal, but it is also not a failure. It is just a moment." I breathe into the discomfort, allowing it to be present without resistance, trusting that it will pass like weather.

- **Action** is choosing to care for myself rather than collapse into the spiral. "I am going to choose rest. Or maybe a walk. Or maybe I will reschedule the hard conversation." This is the conscious choice to respond from clarity, not compulsion.

- **Authenticity** is letting it all be here without demanding resolution right now. "I am allowed to be like this. And it does not make me less." It is the ultimate surrender to impermanence—living from a place of presence where the outside world no longer dictates my inner truth. It is the realization that I am already whole, exactly as I am..

Each step of that process moves me out of reactivity and back into integrity. I am not trying to be perfect; I am trying to be present. This is not a spiritual performance. That is a spiritual practice. One breath at a time.

The Two Wings: Compassion and Wisdom in Action

This is the heart of the Brave Awareness path: we wake up to our own experience, and then we choose to meet it with kindness. We learn to extend that same understanding to others, not because they have earned it, but because we see how deeply they, too, are suffering under the weight of their own human conditioning. Compassion and wisdom are the two essential wings that carry this entire practice into daily life, enabling us to fly through chaos with grace and clarity.

Compassion begins with the ability to see yourself clearly and tenderly. It means understanding without judgment that you are a human being having a human experience. You get mad, glad, sad, scared, and sometimes those feelings are distorted because you are hungry, tired, or hurt. That does not make you broken. That makes you human. We cannot get away from our humanity because everything we experience is filtered through it. And we are not better or worse than that. The real suffering begins when we start measuring ourselves against inhuman ideals, expecting ourselves to be calm all the time, wise all the time, compassionate all the time. We have been taught that the goal is to transcend being human. But the deeper truth is that the path is to befriend it.

And once we stop judging ourselves for being human, we can begin to stop judging others. That is where wisdom comes in. Wisdom is when we extend the same compassionate lens, we have learned to offer ourselves toward others, even the ones we have habitually criticized or condemned. Wisdom is when we realize that *those people doing those things* are mad, glad, sad, scared, hungry, tired, and hurt. Just like us. You stop needing to diagnose everyone who hurt you as a narcissist. You stop needing to label people to make sense of their failings. You stop making someone else's behavior proof of your worth, or lack of it. You start to see people for what they are: humans reacting through the lens of their own conditioning. Just like you. That is where real wisdom is born, not in judging behavior, but in understanding its roots. This embodied understanding is the quiet superpower that transforms daily life, allowing us to meet every challenge, every trigger, every moment of discomfort with a new kind of presence and choice. It means that freedom is not an endpoint; it is a continuous practice of showing up for what is real. It is the active choice to respond with clarity and kindness, even when the world is anything but.

A Commitment to Conscious Living

To live the Brave Awareness path is not to transcend the world. It is to show up for it more fully. To notice what is happening in you and around you. To speak more clearly. To love more wisely. To move more intentionally. It is making the decision, moment by moment, to remain awake, to your pain, your joy, your fear, and your stillness. It is letting yourself be changed by awareness. It is trusting that clarity is enough. It is walking forward, not because you have all the answers, but because you are done pretending you need them in order to begin. This commitment is not a burden; it is the ultimate act of self-love, a daily promise to yourself that you will no longer abandon your own peace for the sake of external validation or fleeting comfort. It is the unwavering decision to live from your deepest truth, even when the path is uncertain.

Final Reflection: Your Life as the Practice

The Brave Awareness path is not a practice you do on the cushion and then forget. It is a way of being. It is how you greet your family when you are tired. It is how you speak to yourself when you fall short. It is how you notice a surge of anger or grief and say, "This, too." It is how you navigate fear, not by pretending you are fearless, but by knowing you are not ruled by fear anymore. Living this way does not make life easier. It makes life more real. More rooted. More honest. And in that honesty, there is room for everything, joy, grief, doubt, hope, silence, and belonging. This is not the promise of a perfect life. It is an invitation to an authentic one. One breath at a time. One return at a time. And you are ready.

Chapter 18: Living the Brave Awareness Path – A Commitment to Conscious Living

This journey through Brave Awareness has unfolded a profound understanding: that peace is not an absence of challenge, but a presence of clarity. We have seen how the hidden master of fear, the illusion of control, and the ceaseless clamor of the mind often dictate our lives, creating cycles of suffering we mistake for our inherent reality. You have learned how the 5A Model, Awareness, Acknowledgment, Acceptance, Action, and Allowing, provides a dynamic compass for navigating these inner landscapes. And in Chapter 16, we explored how compassion and wisdom serve as the two essential wings that lift us beyond reactivity into a space of conscious choice and deeper connection.

Now, as we approach the culmination of these teachings, the question shifts from "what is Brave Awareness?" to "how do I live Brave Awareness?" This chapter is your guide to translating the profound insights you have gained into the practical, moment-by-moment commitment of conscious living. It is not about becoming someone fundamentally different, but about shedding the layers of conditioning that obscure the freedom and wholeness that are already your birthright. The real practice does not begin until you are back in the world, trying to hold your center while stuck in the traffic jam of a messy, beautiful life. It is in the traffic jam, the difficult family dinner, the unexpected email, or the quiet hum of your nervous system that real practice begins. Here, in the ordinary, is where we learn to pause, to notice, and to choose a new way forward, reinforcing the truth that you were never lost, you were simply believing a story.

This commitment to conscious living is an active, ongoing engagement. It is a willingness to meet everything life offers, not with performance or perfection, but with honesty and presence. It is a continuous return to the ground of your being, armed with the understanding that every challenge is an invitation to deepen your awareness and refine your capacity for compassion and wisdom. This chapter will provide you with a powerful, repeatable framework for embodying these truths, making the Brave Awareness path a living, breathing reality in every moment of your day.

The Subtle Symphony of Daily Practice: A Personal Reflection

For decades, my spiritual practice often felt compartmentalized. There was the "on-the-cushion" me – calm, reflective, connected. And then there was the "off-the-cushion" me – capable, driven, but often riddled with a low hum of anxiety when faced with the relentless demands of a busy life. I could deliver a profound dharma talk on impermanence, then get disproportionately irritated by a slow driver on the way home. The insights were there, but the *integration* into the messy reality of everyday human experience felt like a separate, often elusive, challenge.

I remember a recent morning that perfectly illustrated this internal tug-of-war. My husband, Darren, had been working a demanding string of night shifts, getting home at 3 or 4 a.m. I pride myself on being an early riser, and usually, the house is quiet and still for my morning routine of coffee, weighing myself (a small, neurotic but grounding ritual after significant weight loss), and a brief period of reading or meditation. However, on this particular morning, as the sun began to peek through the blinds, I felt a deep ache in my lower back, a lingering stiffness from a particularly vigorous gardening session the day before. Immediately, my mind, ever the efficient problem-solver (and fear-avoider), began its familiar narrative: "Ugh, this is going to be one of *those* days. You are already behind. You should have stretched more. You probably overdid it again."
The discomfort was not just physical; it was mental, tinged with self-criticism and a subtle fear of being "off" for the day. My first impulse,

a deeply conditioned one, was to distract myself. My hand instinctively reached for my phone, ready to scroll through social media, seeking that quick hit of external stimulation to override the internal unease. It is a pattern I have observed countless times: when physical or emotional discomfort arises, my mind seeks an immediate external "soothe."

But this time, a tiny flicker of awareness caught it mid-motion. "Ah," I thought, "this is *the* pattern." Not "I am a failure for feeling this way," or "I need to fix this back pain immediately." Just, "This is the impulse to avoid." I paused, my thumb hovering over the Instagram icon. I felt the stiffness in my back, the slight clench in my jaw, the whisper of self-judgment. And instead of acting on the impulse, I consciously lowered my hand. I took a slow, deliberate breath, feeling my feet on the cool hardwood floor. I affirmed, "This is what it feels like to be human right now. This discomfort is here, and it is okay." It was not a grand, instantaneous transformation. The backache did not vanish, and the urge to scroll still lingered. But in that small, unglamorous moment, I had interrupted a lifelong pattern. I chose to meet discomfort with presence rather than avoidance. Instead of numbing, I noticed. Instead of reacting, I responded. I then chose to gently stretch, poured my coffee, and sat in silence for a few minutes, simply feeling my body and breath, allowing the discomfort to be present without letting it dictate my day. This small return to conscious choice, amidst the ordinary, is the very essence of living the Brave Awareness path. It is in these thousands of subtle pivots that true freedom unfolds.

Companion Practice: A Return to Conscious Choice

You do not need an altar or incense to practice conscious living. You just need a pause, a moment to remember what is real and what is possible. This is a simple, repeatable practice you can do in the space of a single minute or stretch across ten. Use it when you feel off-center. When you are caught in a narrative. When you do not trust your reaction. When you want to come home.
This is the practice of living Brave Awareness.

Step One: Notice Your State

The first act of conscious living is simply to become aware of what is happening, both internally and externally, without immediately jumping to conclusions or trying to change it. This is about cultivating a radical honesty with yourself, peeling back the layers of automatic judgments and stories. When a flicker of discomfort arises, be it a physical sensation, a racing thought, or an emotion like irritation or anxiety, gently bring your attention to it. Ask yourself: "What am I *actually* feeling in this moment?"

Is there tightness in my jaw, shoulders, or gut? Is my mind replaying a past conversation or catastrophizing a future event? Am I feeling a subtle hum of exhaustion, sadness, or a prickle of impatience? Be radically honest without adding a story. You are not diagnosing a problem, fixing a flaw, or escaping an unpleasant sensation. You are simply witnessing.

For example, if you are stuck in traffic and feel irritation rising, instead of immediately thinking, "This is infuriating, I am going to be late," simply notice the physical sensations: "My jaw is clenched. My shoulders are tight. There is a hot flush in my chest." Then, name the emotion without the narrative: "This is frustration." Not "I *am* frustrated because this driver is an idiot," but simply, "This is frustration, arising in my experience." This simple act of noticing creates a micro-pause, a crucial gap between the stimulus and your conditioned reaction. It is the first, most fundamental act of self-compassion: seeing what is truly here without turning away from it.

- *In a tense meeting:* Notice the flush in your face, the racing heart, the urge to interrupt. Just "This is anger."

- *When a loved one says something dismissive,* notice the immediate sting, the thought "I am not valued." Just "This is hurt."

- *Scrolling social media and feeling inadequate:* Notice the comparison, the sinking feeling. "This is envy." "This is self-doubt."

This moment of non-judgmental observation is where everything begins to shift.

Step Two: Affirm the Truth

Once you have noticed your state, the next step is to affirm the truth of that experience with kindness. This is not about positive affirmations that bypass reality; it is about acknowledging your humanity. Place a hand gently on your heart, your belly, or your shoulder, wherever contact feels grounding and supportive. This physical touch can be a powerful anchor, a tangible reminder of your presence and capacity for self-support. Then, whisper or think something true and kind to yourself.

This might be: "This is what it feels like to be human right now." Or "I do not have to fix this feeling; I just have to notice it." You might remind yourself, "Even this belongs," signaling that all parts of your experience, even the uncomfortable ones, are welcome in the space of your awareness. A powerful addition that often resonates deeply is: "Nothing is wrong with me. I am meeting this with awareness." This statement directly counters the common internal narrative of shame and inadequacy that so often accompanies difficult emotions. You are not affirming the *narrative* (e.g., "I am a failure," or "This situation is hopeless"); you are affirming your *presence* and your capacity to be with what is, without judgment.

This step validates your internal experience, creating a felt sense of safety and self-acceptance that begins to loosen the grip of fear and resistance. It is about befriending yourself in the very moment you might otherwise turn away or launch into self-criticism. It grounds you in the understanding that your emotional and physical responses are natural, not flaws.

- *Feeling overwhelmed by your to-do list:* Place your hand on your chest and whisper, "This is what it feels like to be overwhelmed, and it is okay to feel this human experience."

- *After a social interaction where you felt awkward:* Gently touch your face and acknowledge, "This is anxiety about fitting in, and I am meeting myself here."

- *Experiencing chronic pain:* Place your hand on the area and affirm, "This pain is here, and it belongs. I do not have to fight it."

This simple act of internal validation creates the necessary space for true healing and choice.

Step Three: Ask, "What is the Kindest Choice I Can Make Right Now?"

This is the pivotal turning point, the moment where you reclaim your agency. After genuinely noticing your state and affirming its truth with compassion, you are no longer operating from a place of blind reaction. Now, from this grounded space, you can ask yourself: "Given how I am feeling right now, tired, irritated, scared, overwhelmed, what is the most conscious and compassionate thing I can do for myself?"

The answer might surprise you, precisely because it often goes against our conditioned impulses to push, fix, or distract. It might mean choosing:

- **Resting instead of pushing forward:** If you are physically depleted, honoring that need for rest, even if it means

postponing a task, is a profound act of self-care. It is
recognizing that productivity at the expense of your well-being
is not sustainable.

- **Drinking water instead of picking a fight:** Sometimes, our
  reactivity is exacerbated by simple physiological needs like
  dehydration or low blood sugar. Hydration can shift your state
  more fundamentally than engaging in an argument.

- **Saying no instead of people-pleasing:** If you feel overwhelmed
  by a request, a compassionate "no" honors your boundaries
  and energy, preventing future resentment and self-
  abandonment. This is an act of integrity.

- **Taking a walk instead of doom-scrolling:** If your mind is
  spiraling with anxious thoughts or comparison, moving your
  body and connecting with nature can be a more
  compassionate response than passively consuming distressing
  or triggering content.

- **Turning off the podcast and sitting in silence:** If you are
  constantly filling every moment with noise, choosing stillness
  allows your nervous system to regulate and creates space for
  new insights or simply a deeper sense of peace to emerge.

The key here is not to make the "perfect" choice, but to make a
present one. It is about choosing consciously from a place of

awareness, rather than being driven by autopilot, old fears, or external pressures. This subtle but profound shift is the difference between living reactively and living consciously. It is an active decision to align your actions with your deepest well-being, rather than with inherited patterns or the demands of the outer world. This step is where true liberation begins, as you realize you have agency in every moment.

Step Four: Reconnect to Your Breath and Body

Once you have identified the kindest choice, the next step is to embody it. This means dropping back into the immediate, tangible experience of your body and breath to solidify that conscious choice. Take one slow, deliberate inhale, and then an even slower, more spacious exhale. Feel the gentle rise and fall of your chest or belly. Let yourself feel the sensation of your feet on the ground, the solid support of your seat beneath you. Notice any tension melting away with each out-breath, a physical release accompanying your mental shift.

This is not about chasing a feeling of peace; it is about becoming profoundly present to what *is*. You are not trying to get away from the discomfort that initially triggered the practice; you are simply refusing to let that discomfort drive your actions. This step anchors your conscious choice in your physical reality, preventing the mind from immediately spiraling into new narratives or second-guessing your decision. It is a return to your internal steady ground, a physical affirmation that you are here, now, and capable of holding your experience with presence.

For instance, if your "kindest choice" were to take a walk, as you walk, consciously feel your feet hitting the pavement. Notice the rhythm of your breath. Feel the air on your skin. If your choice were to say "no" to an extra task, as you deliver that message, feel your feet on the ground, grounding your words with your physical presence. This simple reconnection can profoundly shift your internal state, providing a sense of calm resilience even when the external situation remains unchanged. It is here that awareness becomes a felt sense, not just a mental concept.

Step Five: Carry It Forward Gently

This practice does not end when you take that final deep breath or get off your metaphorical cushion. It is designed to ripple outward, touching every aspect of your day. The intention is to carry this tone of awareness, compassion, and conscious choice into your next interaction, your next email, your next decision. Let awareness walk with you like a quiet, discerning companion, a gentle internal guide. This means that as you move through your day, you remain subtly attuned to your inner state. If irritation begins to rise during a conversation, you can gently notice it and choose to soften your response rather than escalating. If you feel the pull to distraction, you can pause, reconnect to your breath, and then make a conscious choice about how to use your attention. If you deliver a clear boundary and the other person reacts with defensiveness, you can gently carry forward your commitment to peace, not engaging in their reactivity.

And if you "lose it", if you fall back into an old pattern, react impulsively, or get swept away by a difficult emotion, that is okay. You have not failed. You have simply wandered. The practice then becomes: Notice. Breathe. Choose again. This is how you live awake: not all at once, not in perfect stillness, but in thousands of small, conscious returns to the truth of this moment. It is a continuous, gentle recalibration, an unwavering commitment to your own authenticity and peace, one breath, one choice, one conscious return at a time. The power is not in never straying, but in the unwavering commitment to return. This is the practice of a lifetime.

When to Use This Practice

This "Return to Conscious Choice" practice is a versatile tool for navigating the countless subtle and overt challenges of daily life. Reach for it when you need to recalibrate, recenter, and respond with integrity. Use it:

- **When you are about to have a conversation and you feel off:** Before a difficult meeting, a sensitive family discussion, or even just a casual chat where you feel misaligned or emotionally raw, take a minute to ground yourself and consciously choose your approach.

- **When you are spiraling in comparison, doubt, or disappointment:** When social media triggers inadequacy, or old narratives of "not enough" begin to whisper, use the practice to return to your inherent worth and quiet the internal critic.

- **When you are "doom-thinking" about the future:** When anxiety about what might happen tomorrow or next week starts to consume your present moment, bring yourself back to the here and now, focusing on the kindness you can offer yourself in this very breath.

- **When you feel emotionally raw and do not know why:**
Sometimes, big feelings surface without an obvious cause. This
practice provides a gentle way to acknowledge them without
needing immediate answers or feeling overwhelmed.

- **When you are making a decision but feel disconnected from
yourself:** When faced with a choice, big or small, that leaves
you feeling fragmented or unsure of your inner wisdom, use
the steps to reconnect to your deepest truth and discern your
most authentic path forward.

- **When you notice yourself people-pleasing or abandoning your
boundaries,** use the practice to pause, affirm your needs, and
choose a response that honors your integrity, even if it feels
uncomfortable.

- **When you are caught in a cycle of overthinking or rumination,**
shift your attention from the mental loop to the physical
sensations of your body and the rhythm of your breath,
creating distance from the mind's incessant chatter.

- **When you experience sudden irritation or anger,** instead of
reacting impulsively, apply the steps to understand the
underlying trigger and choose a response rooted in clarity and
self-care.

Let this practice be a gentle reminder: Awareness changes everything. Compassion sustains it. Wisdom emerges when you live from both. That is what it means to walk the Brave Awareness path.

I remain steady in clarity, generous in presence, and devoted to wholeness.

I am allowed to be free.
I am allowed to be clear.
I am allowed to be whole.

Chapter 19: The Unfolding Path - Living Brave Awareness Beyond the Page

As these pages draw to a close, we stand together at a threshold. Not the end of a journey, but the vibrant beginning of one that will unfold, breath by breath, through the tapestry of your own life. This book has been an invitation, a guiding hand through the landscape of Brave Awareness, revealing the profound simplicity and power of conscious living. We have unmasked the subtle architects of suffering, the pervasive whispers of fear, the exhausting illusion of control, the ceaseless clamor of the mind, and the seductive pull of distraction. And in doing so, we have discovered that the peace and freedom you have always sought are not distant destinations, but inherent truths waiting to be remembered within you.

My journey, as you have read, has been a testament to this truth. From the depths of despair and the relentless grip of anxiety to the quiet triumph of recognizing a thought as just a thought, or a pattern as simply a pattern, this path has transformed my existence. It was not a sudden, dramatic awakening that erased all challenges. Instead, it was a slow, deliberate process of noticing, of returning, of choosing presence over autopilot, again and again. My passion for this practical approach stems from the very real, tangible relief it has brought to my own life. I have seen firsthand that true transformation does not require escaping the world or transcending our humanity. It demands a courageous, honest engagement with it, armed with the simple yet profound tools of awareness, compassion, and wisdom. This is why I felt compelled to share this work: because the insights I have gained are not abstract philosophies, but actionable steps that can fundamentally change how you experience every single moment. The true measure of any spiritual path is not found in a retreat hall or on a meditation cushion; it is discovered in the messy, unpredictable, and often unglamorous moments of daily life. It is in the traffic jam, the difficult family dinner, the unexpected email, or the quiet hum of your nervous system that the real practice begins. Here, in the ordinary, is where we learn to pause, to notice, and to choose a new way forward, reinforcing the truth that you were never lost, you were simply believing a story. This commitment to conscious living is an active, ongoing engagement. It is a willingness to meet everything life offers, not with performance or perfection, but with honesty and presence. It is a continuous return to the ground of your being, armed with the understanding that every challenge is an invitation to deepen your awareness and refine your capacity for compassion and wisdom.

The Arc of Awakening: From Fear to Flourishing

Recall the beginning of our journey, where we unmasked the subtle, pervasive presence of fear. Not the obvious terror of physical danger, but the insidious, internal fear that whispers, "I am not enough," "I will never have what I genuinely want," or "I will lose what I love." You learned that this fear, though deeply conditioned for survival, often misfires in our modern world, keeping us trapped in cycles of unnecessary suffering. The Brave Awareness path begins here, by gently pulling these hidden fears into the light, transforming them from unknown experts into recognized patterns. This initial awareness is the spark that allows us to begin seeing these deeply ingrained responses not as flaws, but as signals, invitations to understand ourselves more deeply and choose differently. The liberation that arises from this recognition is profound, allowing you to step out of the reactive loop and into a space of conscious agency.

From that foundation, we journeyed into the illusion of control, the exhausting pursuit of managing external circumstances and internal states, often mistaking vigilance for wisdom. You saw how clinging to what we believe we need to be okay, whether it is a perfect body, a stable career, or constant validation, ultimately leads to fatigue and disconnection. The profound insight emerged that true freedom lies not in dominating life, but in releasing the illusion that we need to. It is in the subtle act of softening, of unclenching, that genuine peace is rediscovered, a peace that does not demand perfect circumstances but arises from profound presence. This understanding liberates vast amounts of energy previously spent in futile striving, redirecting it towards authentic engagement with the present moment. It is the deep exhale after holding your breath for a lifetime, a recognition that the universe is not waiting for you to control it, but to flow with it.

We then explored the pervasive nature of unconscious distraction, recognizing how readily we fill every quiet moment with noise and activity to avoid the discomfort of stillness or the deeper truths within. This led to the radical realization that you are not your mind, not your thoughts, nor your emotions. You are the vast, open awareness that observes them all, like the sky holding the passing weather systems. This distinction is the bedrock of true liberation, empowering you to watch the mind's drama without being consumed by it. It allows you to step onto the steady riverbank of presence, gaining agency not by controlling the river, but by understanding your relationship to it. This profound separation from the incessant mental chatter is not an act of detachment, but one of deep, compassionate self-recognition, allowing you to witness the passing parade of thoughts without identifying with any single float.

The 5A Model, Awareness, Acknowledgment, Acceptance, Action, and Allowing (or Authenticity), became your compass for navigating this inner terrain. You have seen Awareness as the initial spark of noticing, catching patterns before they sweep you away. Acknowledgment is naming what you see without judgment, releasing the illusion that a reaction signifies a failure, much like releasing the idea that a sneeze is a personal failing. Acceptance is the courageous act of softening into what is, dissolving resistance, and allowing emotions to pass like waves. Action is choosing a conscious response from clarity, rather than compulsion, transforming automatic reactions into intentional choices. And allowing as the integration, where this practice becomes a way of being, fostering freedom and presence, and releasing the need for things to be different from what they are. These are not just concepts; they are the living rhythm of a life deeply rooted in truth, a dance between your inner landscape and the world around you, a practical blueprint for navigating the human experience with grace.

We examined the critical role of clear speaking and conscious relationships, recognizing the invisible erosion of self that occurs when compassion becomes self-abandonment. You learned that boundaries are not about punishing others, but about preserving your integrity and peace. This courage to speak your truth, not from anger but from clarity, transforms relationships from arenas of reaction into opportunities for genuine connection. Similarly, the exploration of "Curiosity over Judgment" freed you from the exhausting burden of personalization, revealing that most of what people do reflects their conditioning, not a verdict on your worth. This shift allows you to witness human behavior with a deeper understanding, extending compassion not as an excuse, but as a path to your liberation from suffering. It is in this space of non-judgmental curiosity that true empathy can flourish, transforming your interactions from battles to opportunities for shared humanity and allowing you to hold the complexity of others with an open heart.

Finally, we shattered the myth of happiness as a constant state and the illusion of "more" that often fuels endless craving. You discovered that true peace is not found in getting what we want, but in no longer needing anything to complete us. Radical Neutrality emerged as the liberating middle path, a profound openness to what is, without the compulsion to make it different, allowing you to experience joy and sorrow without clinging to either. This state allows you to stand steady and unmoved, even when the world around you is in chaos, a beacon of inner calm amidst any storm. It is the understanding that fullness is found not in accumulation, but in the spaciousness of simply being, a quiet revolution against the constant demands of desire.

The Art of Return: Your Unfolding Masterpiece

The Brave Awareness path is not a one-time revelation; it is an ongoing practice of return. Life, in its inherent dynamism, will continue to present challenges, trigger old wounds, and invite you to wander from your center. There will be moments when doubt whispers its familiar tales of inadequacy, when the clamor of the world feels overwhelming, or when the intensity of your own emotions threatens to pull you back into unconscious reactivity. This is not failure; it is simply the nature of being human. The journey is not about eliminating these experiences, but about fundamentally changing your relationship with them.

The true strength cultivated through Brave Awareness lies in your capacity to *return.* Each time you notice the subtle tightening of fear, the familiar pull of distraction, or the insidious narrative of self-doubt, you have a choice. You can lean into the practice of returning: taking a conscious breath, placing a hand on your heart, gently naming what you feel, and asking, "What is the kindest choice I can make right now?" This consistent, gentle redirection, from outward grasping to inward presence, from reactive habit to conscious choice, is the very essence of integration. It is the conscious, repeated act of choosing clarity over confusion, and kindness over judgment, both for yourself and for others. This is the quiet, unwavering discipline that builds true inner freedom, a muscle strengthened with every conscious pivot.

It is in these thousands of small, conscious pivots that the path is truly lived. It is the practice of "not fixing, not striving, not manifesting, or chasing, not self-improvement disguised as spirituality. Just noticing. Just breathing. Just returning. Again. And again. And again." Every time you choose to return, you reinforce the profound truth that you were never broken, never lost, you were simply believing in a story that no longer serves your highest truth. This cumulative process builds an unshakable inner ground, a reservoir of peace and resilience that becomes increasingly accessible with each return. It is not about grand gestures, but about the quiet, consistent discipline of presence, a continuous act of self-reclamation, transforming the mundane into the sacred.

This ongoing commitment to conscious living is the ultimate act of self-love. It is a daily promise to yourself that you will no longer abandon your peace for the sake of external validation, fleeting comfort, or the illusion of control. It is the unwavering decision to live from your deepest truth, even when the path is uncertain, even when you do not have all the answers. The path of Brave Awareness makes life not necessarily easier, but *realer*. More rooted. More honest. And in that honesty, there is room for everything: joy, grief, doubt, hope, silence, and belonging. This is the invitation to an authentic life, lived fully and freely, a life where every moment, no matter how ordinary, holds the potential for profound awakening.

Your Life as the Practice, Your Presence as the Teaching

As you step beyond these pages, remember that your life itself is the most profound practice. How you greet your family when you are tired, how you speak to yourself when you fall short, how you notice a surge of anger or grief and say, "This, too", these are the moments where Brave Awareness truly shines. You navigate fear not by pretending to be fearless, but by knowing you are no longer ruled by it. You learn to hold your humanity with tenderness, recognizing that every emotion, every challenge, is an inherent part of the rich tapestry of being alive.

This living integration is your quiet superpower. It means that the freedom you seek is not an endpoint, but a continuous unfolding. It means you are empowered to meet every challenge, every trigger, every moment of discomfort with a new kind of presence and choice. Your embodied presence becomes the most powerful teaching tool you possess. You do not have to convince anyone or preach your truth. You simply live it. And when you live from a place of such authenticity and peace, people notice. Your peace becomes an invitation, not a lecture. It is in the quiet way you handle stress, the calm with which you navigate conflict, the genuine kindness you extend without needing anything in return, that the profound impact of Brave Awareness ripples outward, inspiring those around you to seek their clarity.

The Brave Awareness path invites you to an authentic life. One breath at a time. One return at a time. The ground beneath you is steady. The peace you are seeking is not out there. It is already here. And so are you. You are ready.

May your journey be filled with courage, clarity, and the boundless wisdom that arises from living truly awake.

Brave Awareness Vow: A Living Mantra

*From this moment forward, I respond to life from
Brave Awareness.*

*I honor what I see, speak what is true, and stay rooted in compassion
without abandoning myself.*

*I do not shrink to soothe. I do not over give to earn.
I release the need to be understood by those committed to
misunderstanding.*

*I remain steady in clarity, generous in presence, and devoted to
wholeness.*

*I am allowed to be free.
I am allowed to be clear.
I am allowed to be whole.*

*In every moment.
With every person.
Including myself.*

Appendix A: The Companion Practice for a Return to Conscious Choice

You don't need an altar or incense to practice conscious living. You simply need a pause, a moment to remember what's real and what's possible. This is a simple, repeatable practice you can do in the space of a single minute or stretch across ten. Use it when you feel off-center, when you're caught in a narrative, when you don't trust your reactivity, or when you want to come home. This is the practice of living Brave Awareness.

Step One: Notice Your State. The first act of conscious living is simply to become aware of what is happening, both internally and externally, without immediately jumping to conclusions or trying to change it. When a flicker of discomfort arises, be it a physical sensation, a racing thought, or an emotion like irritation or anxiety, gently bring your attention to it. Ask yourself: "What am I *actually* feeling at this moment?" Is there tightness in my jaw, shoulders, or gut? Is my mind replaying a past conversation or catastrophizing a future event? Be radically honest without adding a story. You are simply witnessing.

Step Two: Affirm the Truth Once you've noticed your state, the next step is to affirm the truth of that experience with kindness. Place a hand gently on your heart, your belly, or your shoulder, wherever contact feels grounding and supportive. Then, whisper or think something true and kind to yourself. This might be: "This is what it feels like to be human right now." Or, "I don't have to fix this feeling; I just have to notice it." A powerful addition is: "Nothing is wrong with me. I am meeting this with awareness."

Step Three: Ask, "What's the Kindest Choice I Can Make Right Now?" This is the pivotal turning point. After genuinely noticing your state and affirming its truth with compassion, you are no longer operating from a place of blind reaction. Now, from this grounded space, you can ask yourself: "Given how I'm feeling right now, tired, irritated, scared, overwhelmed, what's the most conscious and compassionate thing I can do for myself?" The answer might be resting instead of pushing, drinking water instead of picking a fight, or taking a walk instead of doom-scrolling.

Step Four: Reconnect to Your Breath and Body. Once you've identified the kindest choice, the next step is to embody it. This means dropping back into the immediate, tangible experience of your body and breath to solidify that conscious choice. Take one slow, deliberate inhale, and then an even slower, more spacious exhale. Feel your feet on the ground, the solid support of your seat beneath you. This step anchors your conscious choice in your physical reality, preventing the mind from immediately spiraling into new narratives.

Step Five: Carry It Forward Gently. This practice doesn't end when you take that final deep breath. It's designed to ripple outward, touching every aspect of your day. The intention is to carry this tone of awareness, compassion, and conscious choice into your next interaction, your next email, your next decision. And if you "lose it", if you fall back into an old pattern, react impulsively, or get swept away by a difficult emotion, that's okay. You haven't failed. You've simply wandered. The practice then becomes: Notice. Breathe. Choose again.

Appendix B: The Daily Practice of Calling Out What Is

The Intention: This is a quiet, courageous act of radical honesty. The goal is to build the muscle of seeing one true thing each day without the need to fix it, change it, or immediately attach an emotion or story to it. It is the practice of finding the relief that comes from simply acknowledging, "It is like realizing that things get wet when it rains."

The Practice (To be done once a day):

Find a quiet moment. Place a hand on your heart to anchor yourself in your own presence. Take one slow, deep breath.

Then, follow these simple steps:

1. **The Question:** Ask yourself this single, gentle question: **"What is one true thing I can bravely call out today?"**

2. **The Naming:** Let the answer arise without force. When it does, name it as simply and neutrally as possible, without adding a story or a judgment. Here are some universal examples:

- o *"Today, I am calling out the truth that I feel a sense of loneliness."*

- o *"Today, I am calling out the truth that I am avoiding a difficult task."*

- o *"Today, I am calling out the truth that I am comparing myself to someone else."*

- o *"Today, I am calling out the truth that I am proud of a small choice I made."*

- o *"Today, I am calling out the truth that my body is feeling tired and needs rest."*

3. **The Noticing:** After you have named the truth, simply pause. Your only job now is to notice what arises in response. An emotion might surface, such as sadness, fear, or relief. A physical sensation might appear as tightness in your chest, a softening in your shoulders. A thought might try to create a story. Your practice is not to follow these reactions, but to simply notice them with the same neutral awareness:

- o *"Ah, there is sadness arising."*

- o *"There is the pattern of fear."*

- o *"That is a thought about what this means." You are not the feeling. You are the one who is aware of the feeling.*

4. **The Release:** Take one more deep breath and, as you exhale, release the need for the truth to be any different than what it is. You can close the practice with this simple affirmation:

"This is not a failure. It is not a success. It is just what is."

If these words felt like a hand on your back, please consider leaving a review. Your honest feedback helps others who are seeking a way to be okay when life isn't to find this compass.

The path doesn't end here. Join Ronn on the **Brave Awareness Podcast**, or visit BraveAwareness.com for news on retreats and workshops.

Follow Ronn on Instagram

ronnmeditates